Analog Photography

A Beginner's Guide

by

Bo Belvedere Christensen

Other books by the same author (only english titles):

Baruntse - above 7000 meters in the Himalayas, BoD 2011
Poor Kathmandu, BoD 2015
Everest Basecamp Trek - via Gokyo and Cho La, BoD 2020
Annapurna Basecamp Trek - via Ghorepani and Poon Hill, BoD 2020
Panoramic Images - directly on camera, BoD 2021
Baltoro and K2 Basecamp Trek - via Ghondogora La, BoD 2022

Publisher: BoD – Books on Demand, Hellerup, Danmark
Print: BoD – Books on Demand, Norderstedt, Tyskland
Cover: Great Trango in the Karakoram range of the Himalayas after a snow storm. Shot on Nikon F90X using a Tamron 300mm telephoto lens.
ISBN: 9788743033899

Analog Photography

A Beginner's Guide

by

Bo Belvedere Christensen

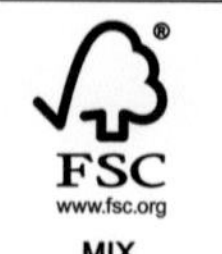
FSC
www.fsc.org
MIX
Papir fra
ansvarlige kilder
Paper from
responsible sources
FSC® C105338

INDHOLD

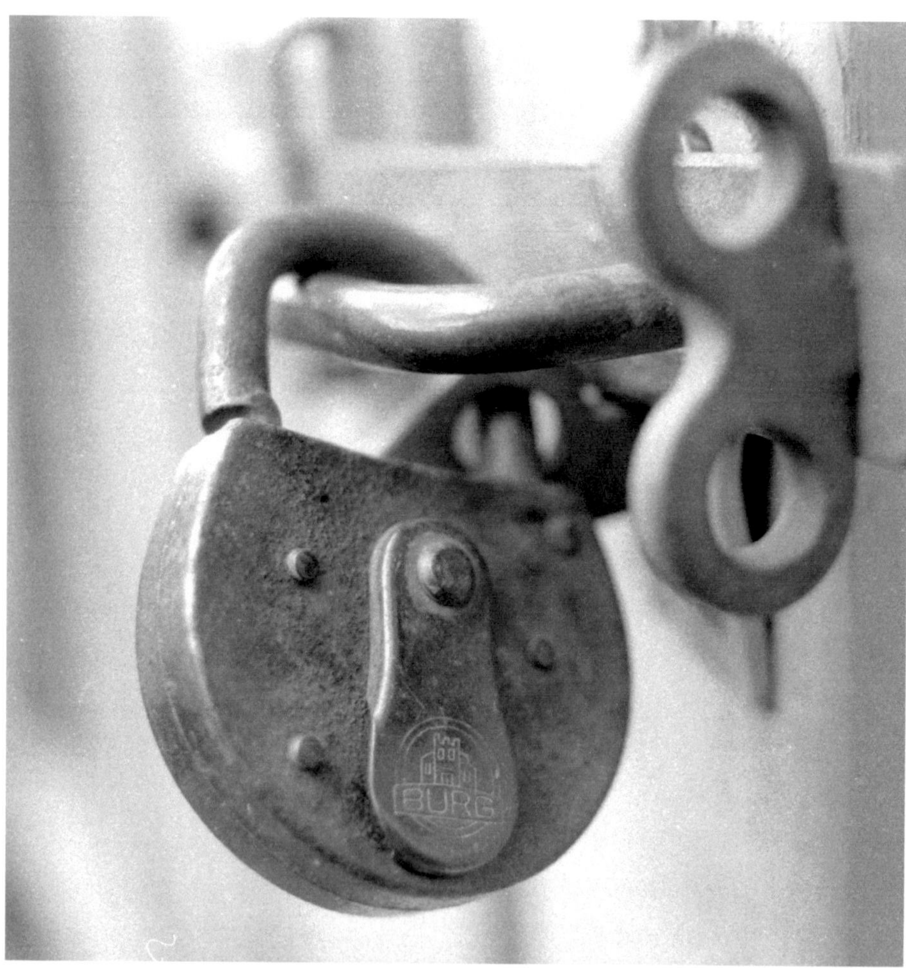

The lock to our back yard. Shot with a Ricoh KR-10X SLR and a 50mm lens, with the ability to focus close up. The film is a Kodak Tmax 100 film, giving a fine grained image. Nevertheles, the beautiful grain structure of the film adds to the attraction of the image.

Preface and basics on analog vs. digital

Most people photographing using any kind of digital photography, that be a real camera or a mobile phone, will be reviewing their images on some kind of screen.

Already here the fundamental difference between analog and digital photography appears. Using a film based camera, you will have no screen to review you images, and you must wait until you film has been developed, you receive printed images, or receive a scan in order to see images on a computer screen.

Off course, you can go all-in and begin to develop yourself. It is actually not that difficult, but it requires some utensils. It will make it possible, as I often do, to photograph early in the day, develop in the middle of the day, and scan or enlarge images later the same day. There is something magical about opening the development tank and having a first look on the results - most often as negatives.

As opposed to the SD or other storage cards used in digital photography, your analog results require film as storage media. That is where some of the charm in analog photography resides, and where the attraction of analog has attracted so many photographers in recent years, maybe not going 100% analog, but at least for a major part of their photography. I would be lying if I said, I don't use digital cameras, and I do appreciate that part of my photographical work.

The fact is, where I am most inspired, and where the best results emerge,

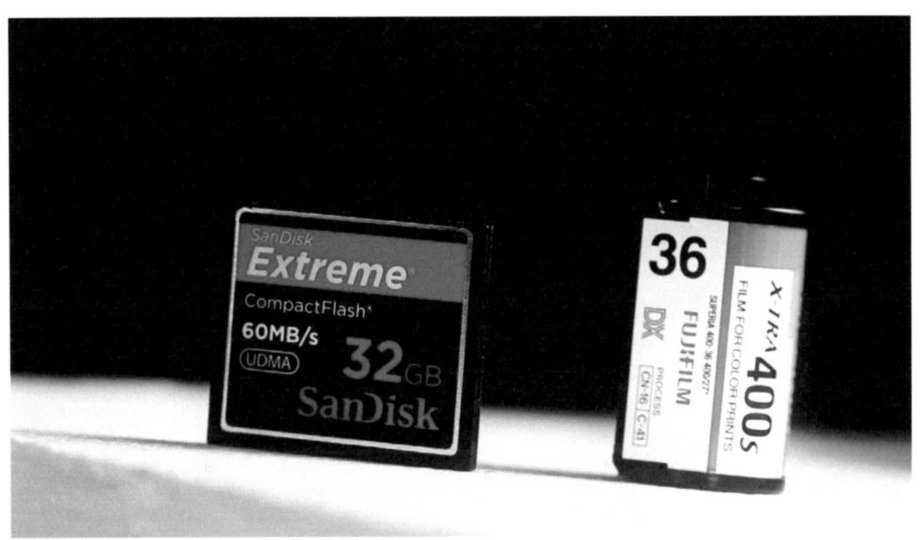

is with film. Especially, I like the look of film, the structure, and the more natural look as opposed to the more clinical, correct, but also a bit plasticky look of digital. Furthermore, depending on the film you choose, this look is different.

Many has tried to mimic the texture of film in post proces with digital images, but to my eyes the results are not satisfying. Where I found a close hit is using the build in film simulations in the mirrorless cameras from Fujifilm. It is also obvious, that Fujifilm with their cameras try to simulate the

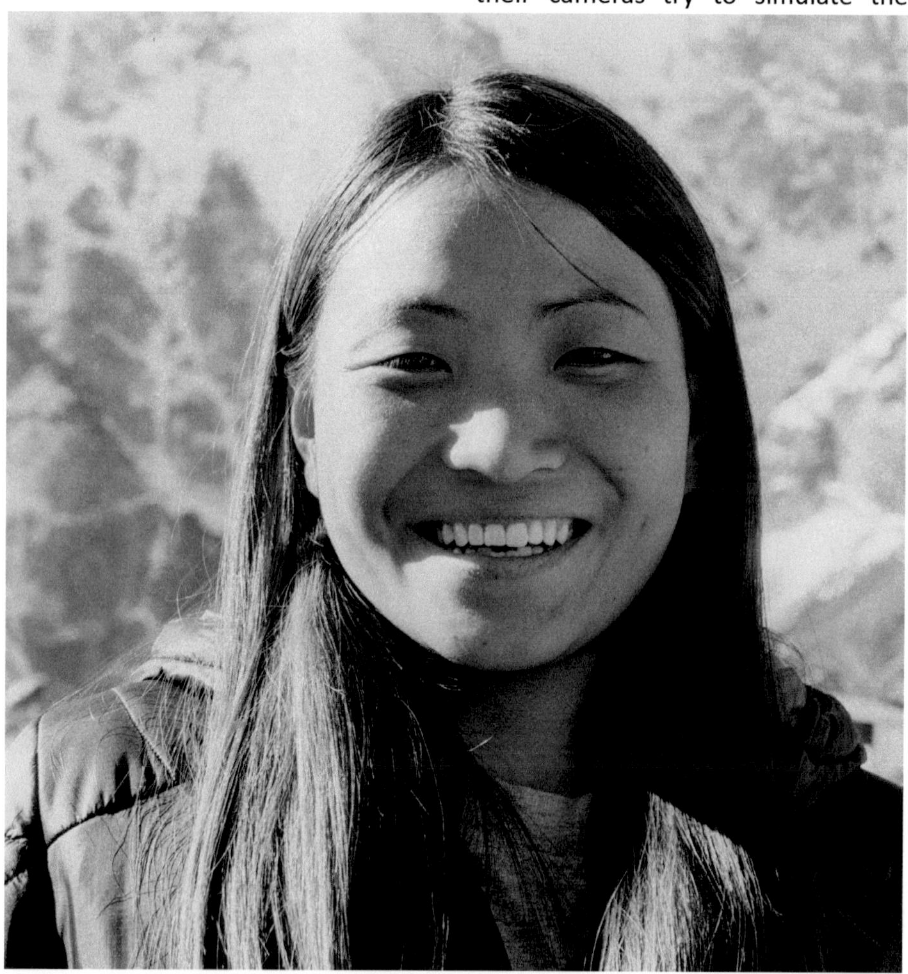

During one of my many treks in the Mount Everest region I shot this portrait of a Sherpani (a female belonging to the ethnic group of sherpas).

I love the grainy structure of the image, that for me gives more life to the image. The camera was a Canon AE-1 SLR with a 50mm f1.4 lens, and the image was shot on Fomapan 100 film.

feel of old style cameras and their operation. Anyhow, although I like the cameras from Fujifilm, I prefer the complete analog proces at least until I have developed the film. After that I usually scan the images and thus turns to digital treatment of the images. Even here one could choose to go all-in, and set up a darkroom, or use one that's is already there e.g. at a school, a photo club, or somewhere else.

Even if you scan the images to you computer, there is often a big difference.

Using a digital camera, we often shoot a lot of images, far more than we would with the limited length of a 36 frame film would pose (depending on the format of film it can be a lot less frames), and also due to the cost of photographing on film.

In itself it makes a huge difference choosing from hundreds if not thousands of images, compared to the images from a single film or maybe a couple.

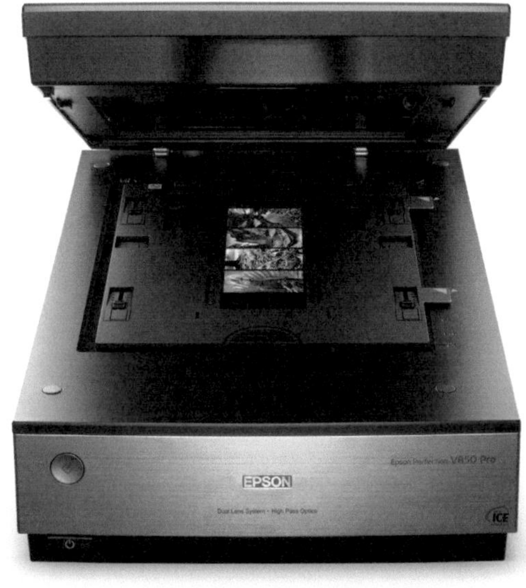

I use several different scanners in order to get my images from analog film into the computer. The above Epson V850 works for image formats from 24x36 and up to 8x10" large format.

It makes post processing much simpler. At the same time, I know from my own workflow and from other photographers I know, that we typically don't spend as much time in post proces on the analog

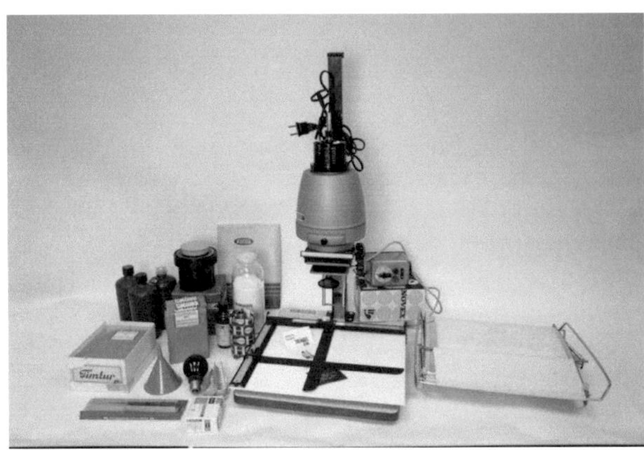

Darkroom equipment hasn't been used for years, but more and more are resuming darkroom work together with the new wave of analog photography. Naturally, not everyone has room and opportunity to have a darkroom, and thereby work completely analog all the way from exposure to print.

Many are more interested in posting on social media, and that in the end requires digital images

images. Images often have exactly the expression, you seek, directly from development and scanning. There is not so much more to do, except maybe cleaning some dust and other impurities, but not so much with regard to contrast, light levels, color balance, and other settings that we manipulate a lot, when we work with the digital camera.

To me both the strength and attraction of analog photography is buried here. What do I want as a photographer? To be out creating with my camera, or sitting by my computer and pulling sliders in Lightroom? I LOVE walking around with my camera, and I wish to minimize the time behind the computer screen. I prefer to work harder to produce the results directly in camera, and that is more often the result when I use an analog camera. Those that swear by their digital cameras say exactly this, that they know the results are perfect, they have seen it on the lcd screen of the camera. I know from myself that I tend to spend huge amounts of time tweaking different parameters for my digital images, as digital imagery encourages perfection, while analog photography encourages you to think more artistically. This is exactly what makes me love analog photography.

One last thing, that always fascinates me, is the partly uncontrollable part

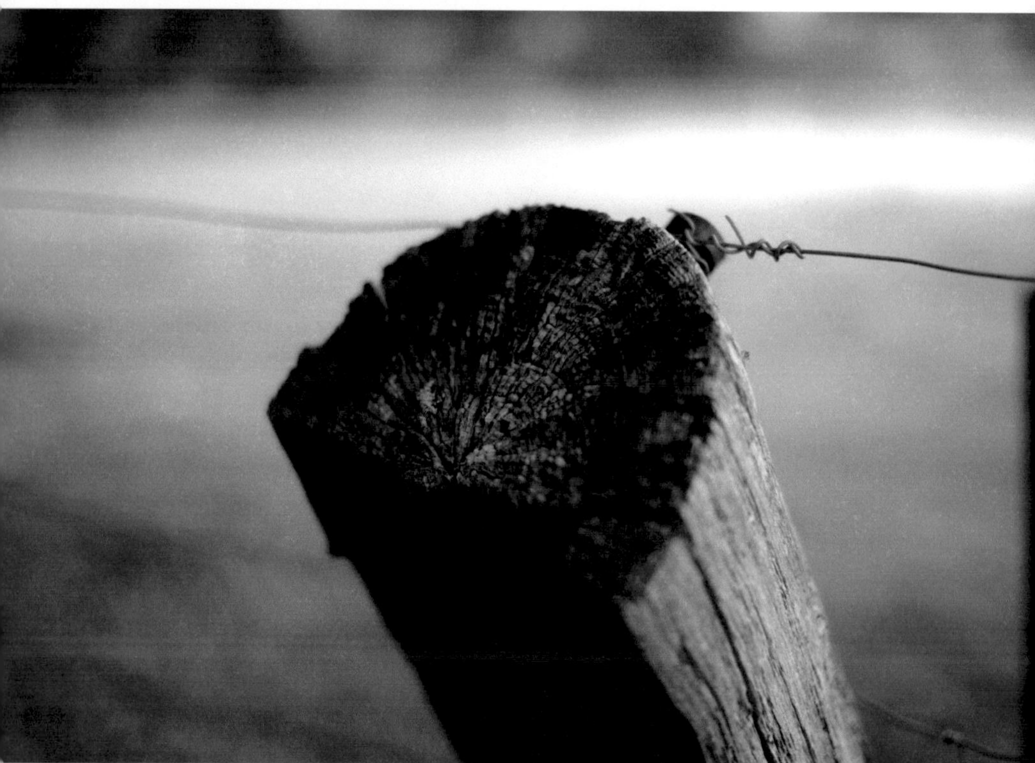

of photography, that partly spawns from the fact, that you can't see the result immediately on the backside of the camera. That part can be driven even further with experimental photography, which of course can also be pursued with digital photography. But is hard to create the look of expired film in post, and that can give some wild results bordering to abstract art. Sometimes I even utilize development processes for film in others ways than they are meant. For instance I sometimes use chemicals for different films than they are meant for, like when I "cross-develop" my color film and develop color positive film in chemicals for color negative film, or the opposite. It can also be development of black and white film, where the film is pushed, which makes the film more sensitive but also influences the contrast and grain structure of the film. That can give some incredible results. Actually, there is a whole book on alternative processes, that has enough experiments to do for a whole life time.

Clearly there is enough to work on, when we are going the analog way, there are lots of opportunity to express yourself creatively. Therefore, I understand fully why so many have chosen to photograph on film even in their professional work. And in this preface I have only covered a fraction of the huge amounts of possibilities to express yourself artistically and experimentally with analog photography.

I wish you a creative and eventful journey into analog photography, and I hope this book can help you through the initial challenges of choosing camera(s), film, and find your own style.

Holte, Denmark, February 2022

Bo Belvedere Christensen

What you need to know from the start

Supposing you haven't already chosen a camera, I'll describe the different kind of cameras available, have a look at specific functions, that some cameras have, and finally show some directions in which to grow as a photographer with the camera of choice.

If you have a camera, you might consider the upgrade path, or you might wonder what lens could provide another expression, than you have previously achieved. This book will also help you in that respect.

Owning a camera but being completely new to photography, except for the one in your mobile phone, there is a lot of necessary basic knowledge, you need to get into. Making your camera ready might require you to insert batteries, load film correctly, mount the lens correctly, choose a suitable camera mode etc.

You also need to get a basic knowledge of analog film, cause unlike on the digital camera the film must suit the situation, you plan to shot in. Though you are not completely locked once the film is chosen, but knowing somewhat on the specifics of the film enables you to know how much you can stretch the film.

We'll have a dive into how to get your images sharp and correctly exposed, as this can require more from you unless you have chosen camera with automatic modes for both focus and exposure. Actually, if you haven't already chosen a camera, I would suggest to avoid cameras that has to much electronics. You'll learn much more by getting in control of focus and exposure right from the start.

Nevertheles, if you have chosen an automatic camera, many of these have the possibility to switch to fully manual control. You should try this!

Then, haven shot you first film, you need to get it out of the camera without spoiling the images, that means it has to be return spooled into the cassette before removing it from the camera. After that you can have it developed at a lab - if you haven't chosen to go all the way and develop yourself, which isn't to hard once you got the right remedies - though this is outside the scope of this book.

Finally, we'll have a look into different shooting situations like portrait, landscape, action etc. These sections detail the specific requirements for each situation, in order to maximise you outcome.

Film types and formats

Through time a bunch of different film formats has been used. Part of these has been replaced and have disappeared completely, while others have existed almost since the birth of photography. We will have a look at the most important, so you are aware of them, even though focus in this book is on the most utilized format, and the one that will be the reference point in this book, the 35mm film also named 135 film.

There are several types of film for this format, where the primary here will be black and white sometimes abbreviated b/w and the color negative film. I'll briefly touch upon color positive film, that had its heyday when we all used slide projectors and showed our images from the holiday on a big screen or on a white wall. Apart from these three types, there are some specialized film, that can be used in certain situations. I have for instance used infrared film, that as its name indicates is sensitive to that extreme part of the red spectrum of light, that we can't see with our eyes. Furthermore, I have used X-ray film, that previously was used to investigate bone fractures or our teeth. Infrared and X-ray films are fascinating to experiment with, and they give amazing results, but they won't be treated further in this book.

Three different film types, two still alive and well, and one thas has been abandoned. To the left the "professional" 120 film, in the middle the most used filmtype, the 135 film also named 35mm due to the width of the film. To the right the APS casette, a film type that only existed for a short period, and now is gone.

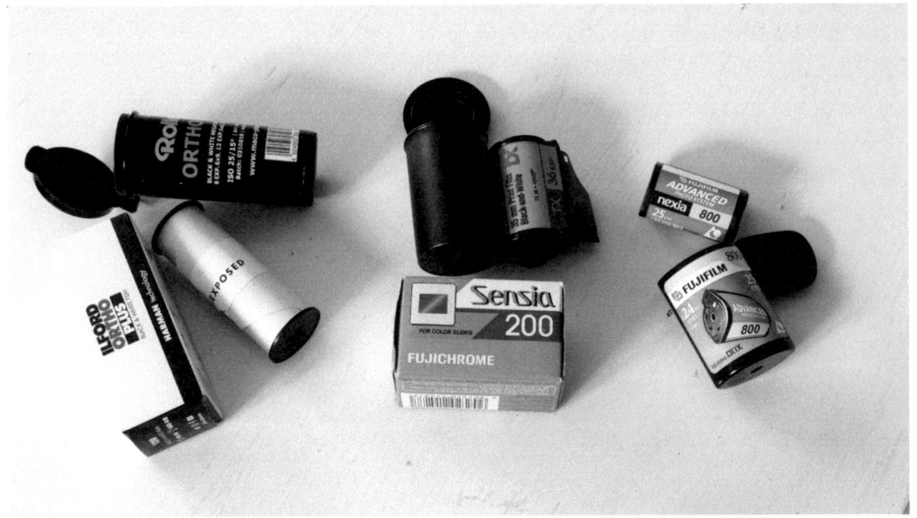

As its name indicates, the 35 mm film is 35 mm wide, it has perforation in both side (sprockets), that insures the film is rolled forward precisely one frame at the time - unless you consciously want something different to happen, for instance when working with double exposures.

Usually, film is bought in single packages containing one film cassette with 36 or 24 exposures, provided you are photographing in the most usual 24x36mm format. There are other frame sizes like "half-frame" that uses 18x24mm for each exposure. There are also specialized panoramic cameras, that expose a larger image frame. I have for instance a camera that exposes frames of 24x72mm, and in fact I have written a whole book on panoramic photography. If that has spurred your interest, you can look it up in the bibliography. In this book for beginners, I will concentrate on the usual 24x36 image frame.

The 126 casette

A film format that had its heyday in the 60s, 70s and 80s is the 126 format. It also uses a 35mm wide film, just like the 135 format, but it was contained in a cassette containing both the source spool and the take up spool, giving the advantage that you don't need to return spool the film. Contrary to 135 it has only sprockets in one side. The image size was actually 28x28 mm, but most cameras only exposed 26x26 mm. Behind the film was a paper layer with numbering, visible through a small hole on the cassette and the camera. Furthermore, the film had holes that indicated the film sensitivity to the camera.

Therefore, it was a format that made it extremely easy for the user, but wasn't intended for professional use. The cameras was also relatively simple point and shoot cameras, even though there was a few more

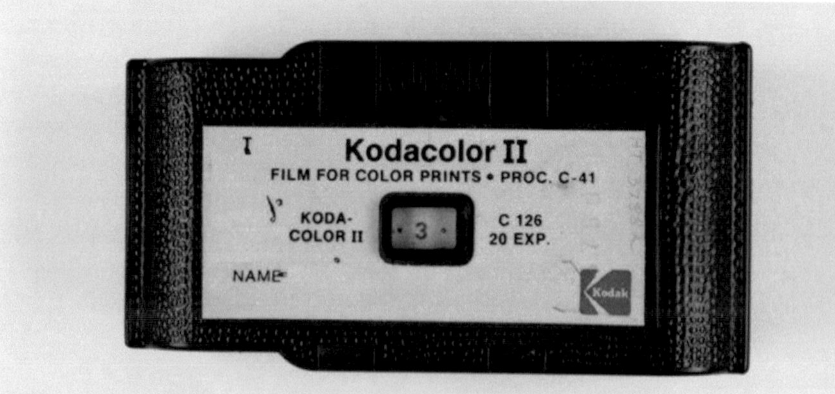

sofisticated models giving the user more control. No matter how fascinating it is to shoot on this format, where only expired films are available as production stopped in 2008, it is not a format to grow with, and furthermore outside the scope of this book. For some serious experimental work it is hereby mentioned.

The APS casette

A format that flourished in a very short period was APS film. It you know a little about digital photo, you might think it's a digital format. Truly, they existed concurrently in the beginning of digital photography, but it is a film format, its name an abbreviation of Advanced Photo System. The size is almost identical to the APS digital sensor, but it was complicated by the fact that you could expose three different size images on the same camera, and even on the same film casette.

This format had a short life span, which, among other things, is due to the extremely advanced system required for film labs to develop and make enlargements. It was overtaken by the digital photography, and only existed from 1996 until both Kodak and Fuji stopped production in 2011.

One major advantage of the APS format was, that the cameras would be made very compact.

You can still buy lots of expired film and used cameras, and I have worked a lot with the format. It has another advantage; most cameras make it possible to change film mid roll as the casette stores information on how many images you have shot.

Unfortunately, there are few places to have the film developed, and I have done it myself, which is a rather

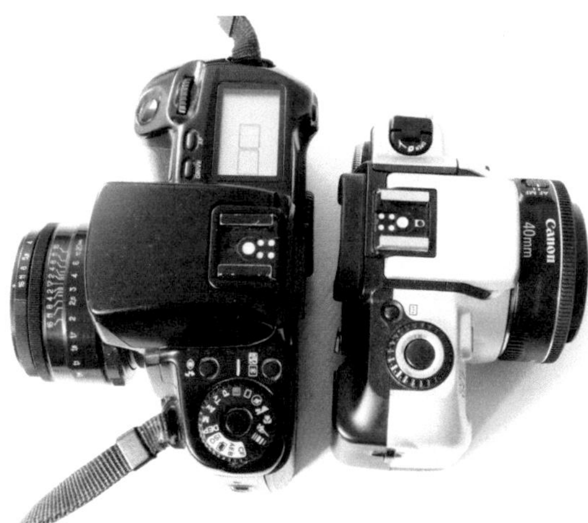

A comparison between a typical single lens reflex (SLR) camera for the 135 film format, a Canon EOS 100, and the far smaller SLR for APS film, a Canon EOS IX7.

Not many SLR cameras were produced for the APS format, but the comparison clearly shows how much the size of the camera could be reduced due to the compact size of the very smart film format.

Most of the APS cameras - by far - are point-and-shoot cameras, also they very compact, but at the same time often having relatively advanced features.

involving proces. Everything is very complicated, and that is probably one of the reasons it has disappeared from the market, contrary to many of the other formats I cover here. Now you have heard about it, but I won't cover it more, except I'll just mention that I'm working on a book about APS film photography, but it is outside the scope of this book.

120 film

A considerably larger image format is obtained by 120 film (previously also 220 film, the same film in double lengths), which today is used in larger and typically professional or semiprofessional cameras.

Initially this format was used in simple box cameras, which was the most common camera type in the first half of the 19th century. In fact it is one of the most long lived film formats, as it has existed since 1901, and is still in production.

The film format supports several different image sizes eg. 4,5x6 cm, 6x6 cm, 6x7 cm, and 6x9 cm.

But there are also here some panoramic formats, of which I have use 6x12 cm, and in a couple of my pinhole cameras even 6x17 cm - a gigantic image format, that I can only utilize as scanned images, as I haven't got an enlarger capable of this huge format. You can see examples of these images in my book on panoramic photography. Now you are informed about this format, but it's to professional to fit within the scope of this book.

Below is my old Agfa Synchro Box camera together with a camera, that most people have heard about, the fantastic Hasselblad 500CM. I'we had a Hasselblad for more than 40 years, and have always loved to photography with it. To me it is one of the ultimatively most inspiring cameras to use.

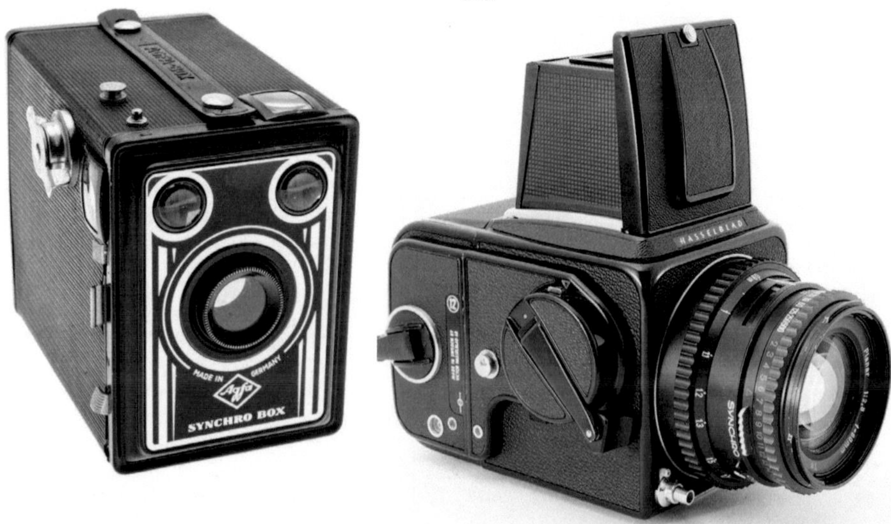

Large format

Large format is crazy fascinating, in fact where it all started in photography early in the 18th century. There are several image formats, some of which are gigantic, but the most used sizes today is 4x5 inches (also written as 4x5", which is app. 10x12.5 cm), 5x7 inches (app. 13x18 cm), and 8x10" (app. 20x25 cm). When I scan a 4x5" in high resolution, I end up with images that are measured not in Megapixels but in Gigapixels. There are no ordinary digital cameras that come even close to the crazy high resolution you obtain with these formats. Obviously, there is a lot of proces time for each image; setting up for the single shoot, development in small batches, and scanning for the individual image. Furthermore, the cameras have a crazy amount of things you can tweak and control for a specific result during the shooting.

Now you know about this extreme format within analog photography, I won't treat it further in this book, even though it might be the most fascinating photography media.

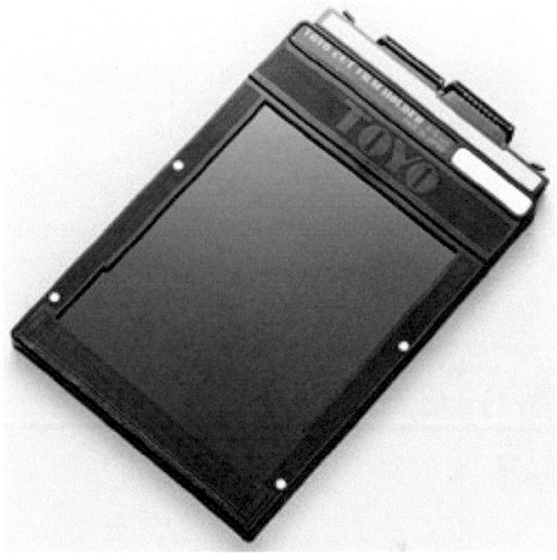

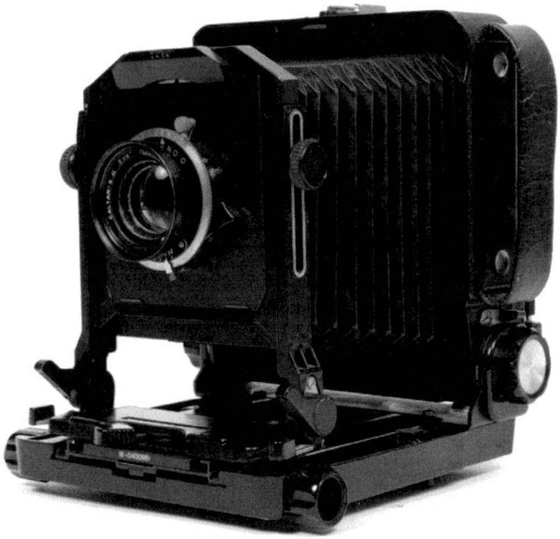

Above is a film holder for the 4x5 inch format. There is an image below a socalled "dark slide" on both sides of the casette. Thus, you have to shots available, but of course you can take several casettes along on a shoot.

To the left is my "portable" collapsible large format camera, a Toyo Field 45A, that weighs in at 2.5 kilo including the lens. It can be collapsed to a box of app. 20x20x10 cm.

It takes around 2-3 minutes to make the camera ready, and put it on a tripod, but especially setting the focus and the huge amount of displacements can take anything from a few minutes to half hours.

Large format photography is for the demanding photographer willing to sacrifice a lot of time for every individual image. In return photography becomes a meditative process.

Comparison of film formats

If you get the opportunity to shoot on several film formats, you will discover that sharpness, and visibility of film grain depends largely on the film format. Therefore, I give you this comparison of film formats, so you know what awaits you, if you one day are utilizing several different film formats.

Image size	Film	Area
18x24mm	135-halfframe	$432mm^2$
17x30mm	APS	$510mm^2$
24x36mm	135-full frame	$864mm^2$
4.5x6cm (645)	120	$2352mm^{2}$*
6x6cm	120	$3136mm^{2}$*
6x7cm	120	$3752mm^{2}$*
4x5 inch	4x5”	$12500mm^2$
8x10 inch	8x10”	$50000mm^2$

***4.5x6 is actually 42x56mm, 6x6 is actually 56x56mm, 6x7 is actually 56x67mm.**

A small selection of film sizes compared. You clearly see the huge difference from the smallest formats like Half Frame (18x24mm), APS (17x30mm), and traditional 35mm (24x36mm in the digital world named ”Full Frame”) to formats using 120 film, like 645 (56x42mm), 6x6 and 6x7. Furthermore, the enourmouslyl arge 4x5” and 8x10” formats are not included.

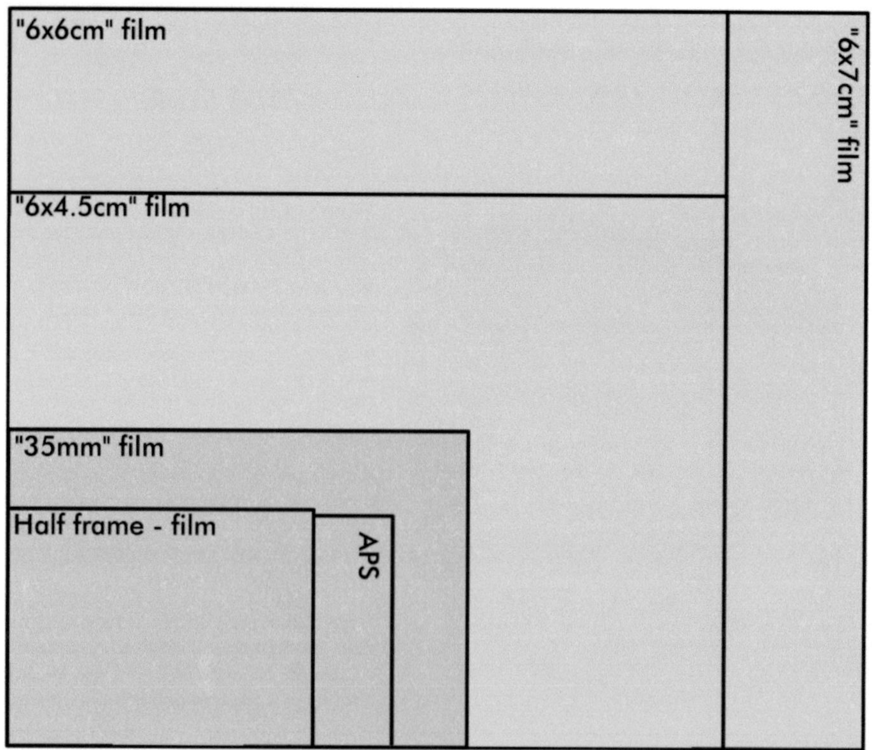

Film sensitivity

If you have used a digital camera, that is not a mobile phone, you maybe know you can set the sensitivity to light. So you set the camera different in bright light as compared to dark situations or even night photography. Most photographers use the automatic settings, and are not aware of the camera adapting the sensitivity according to the available light.

When using film the choice is entirely yours as a photographer, you are forced to decide the sensitivity of the film already when you are buying it - even though, if you develop yourself, you can push the film to larger sensivity, in order to use it in weaker light than it's originally designed for. It has some effects like more visible grain and increased contrast. Conversely, you can also pull the film, as it is called, for lesser sensitivity, resulting in finer grain and lower contrast. With the analog camera, you take a creative choice. In the digital world, increasing the sensitivity does not lead to grain but to ugly looking noise. That is very unlike film grain, that can add a very beautiful artistic element.

The sensitivity in modern film is specified with an ISO value, and usual values are between ISO 50, like the very fine grained Ilford Pan F, and ISO 3200, like Kodaks Tmax P3200 with lots of visible grain and rather high contrast.

All that is very theoretical, so let's take some examples.

You want to take images in bright day light, and you want the results to have small, fine grain that doesn't dominate you motive. In this situation you could choose a film of ISO 50 or 100. These film typically also provide rather low contrast, but it differs from

The image below is almost free of any grain structure as it is shot on 120 film using a 6x17cm piece, and it is shot on ISO 100 film. By the way it is shot using a pinhole camera providing a lovely softness.

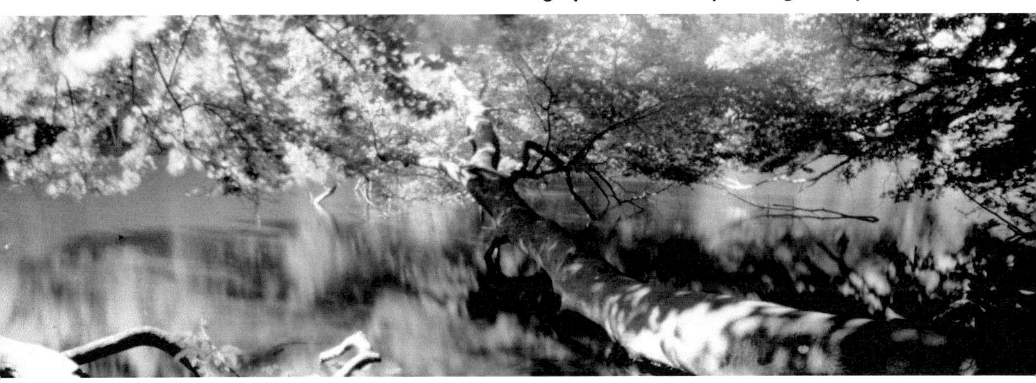

manufacturer to the other. There is a lot of choices, but it would come too far, if I should list all the choices and their characteristics. You must learn that from own experience along the way.

Another scenario is, that you want visible grain structure, so that the film look is obvious from the images. You might also want a bit higher contrast. You might choose a film in the middle territory, like a film of ISO 400, or maybe even higher. Thereby, you will achieve visible grain, but you will also be limited in shooting with fully open aperture in bright day light. We will look into what the effect of that is, when we delve into background sharpness (depth of field).

One last advice concerning choice of film is, from the beginning pick a single or at most two different black and white film, and maybe additionally a color film. Experiment with these in order to learn their characteristics well. If you shoot a new film every time, your experiments want give you the experience, you could have. When you have used one or a few films for a number of shoots, you will end up knowing how the film reacts to different scenarios and settings, and you will be better prepared to achieve the best, when you add a new film to your selection. I would advice you to keep a diary or logbook of your experiments, as that enables you to better judge what combinations creates the images, you are most proud of.

When you have enough experience with you first films, the introduction of new film will probably provide you with quite different results. You will find that they react differently to changes in light and other settings, and, if you go that far, how development can drastically change the film behaviour. Having a logbook will work as a "database" of what works for you, and what doesn't give the results, you like.

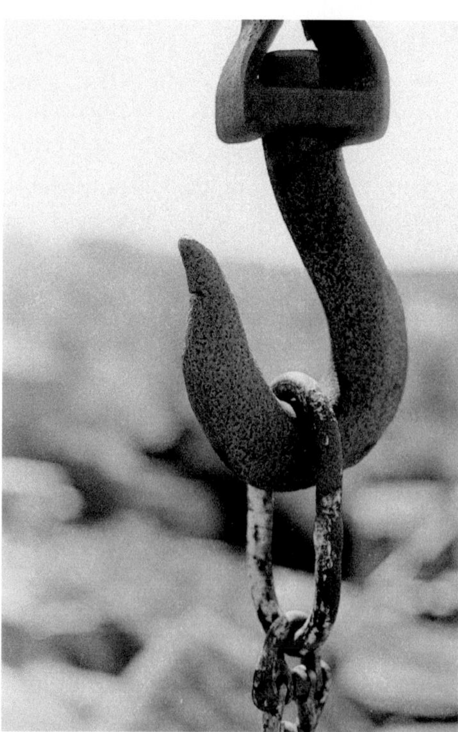

The image is shot on 135 film in the 24x36 format on a ISO 400 film, and shows visible grain structure. The natural choice here was to let the grain of the film accentuate the dated look in the rusty metal hook in an abandoned quarry.

Camera types

In this book I'll cover the use of three main types of camera:

Single Lens Reflex cameras (SLR)

Rangefinder cameras

Compact and point & shoot cameras

Add to this a bunch of camera types, that are very different, and will not be treated, as I don't consider them relevant for the beginner - but certainly very exciting to use once beyond the initial start. It could be cameras like TLRs cameras, Twin Lens Reflex, and pinhole cameras. Do note that the SLR camera can easily be converted to a pinhole camera, nevertheless it is outside the scope of this book, no matter how interesting this kind of photography is.

I will treat a couple of cameras in the experimental category, but only briefly as they, unlike most of the cameras I describe in detail, don't necessarily deliver sharp and correctly exposed results. They are more oriented to the photographer, who wants to do some artistic experiments.

I can begin with an overall advice, if you don't want to spend to much getting started. Go for the lesser known brands. They are just as good as the well known brands, sometimes even better. What I consider known brands are: Canon, Nikon, Minolta, Pentax, Olympus, and the crazy expensive end Leica. Additionally, be aware that the well known brands didn't always produce their own cameras. One of the lesser known producers often delivering cameras,

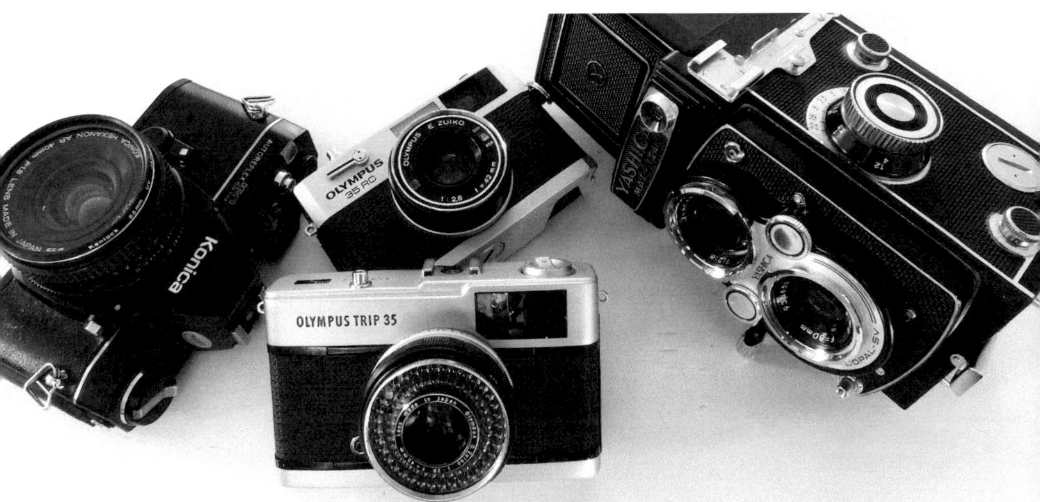

that were rebranded by the well known brands, are Cosina. They have during long time produced cameras for all the high end brands as well as some lesser known like Praktica, Petri, Chinon, and even the highly regarded brand Voigtländer, a name that they achieved the rights for in 1999. By all this I'll convey the message, that quality is not bound to the known brands, and you will often get more bang for the buck with a lesser known brand.

Single Lens Reflex

Single Lens Reflex or abbreviated SLR has, as its name indicates, an image that is reflected from the lens into the viewfinder. That means what you see through the viewfinder is also the view that will hit the film, and you can compose and set focus with great precision. The moment you press the shutter button, the mirror flips away, blocking your view, and making it possible for the light to hit the film. Nevertheless, the film is still blocked by the shutter, that activates microseconds after the mirror flips away, making the exposure of the film. As soon as the shutter closes, the mirror flips back in place, in order for you to see your motive again.

This description covers the majority of SLR cameras, but there are exceptions. For instance on some older cameras the mirror doesn't return automatically after taking the image. When you advance the film, the mirror finally returns to its position, so you again can see through the viewfinder. Another type of exception is more rare as implemented in the Canon EOS RT. This camera has a semi transparent mirror, that does not move away on exposure. You can see through the viewfinder all the time, no so-called "black-out," but that also means less light is hitting the film. An advantage is, that there is no "mirror slap" that can cause shake and image blur.

One commonality of all SLRs is, that the lenses can be changed. That give the opportunity to uses lenses from the most extreme wideangle lenses like the so-called fish eyes, that results in a round image, and where you must be aware not to get your own hair in the frame, to the most powerful telephoto lenses, that make even distant objects seem very close.

These characteristics are not the only thing the swappable lenses can provide, as the lenses provide a huge part of the "filmic look" of you images. There are a huge amounts of lenses, that each provide their own special rendering of your motive. Through the years I have tested hundreds of different lenses, and I still frequently publish new test reports on my homepage. Once in while, I am still astonished by one of these forgotten gems, that a company has produced a long time ago. Some of these lenses are so special, that they only fit one specific type of photography eg. portrait, but are unsuited for anything else. That is the case when photography is not a question of creating a digital, clinical one to one copy of the scene in front of you. When you work creatively with your photography, certain lenses can impose a new style to your work. That is wildly fascinating.

But enough about what SLR is, and why it is such an amazingly flexible tool, that make it possbile to continue your photographic journey even after - in my case - almost 60 years of photography.

SLR camera examples

Cosina CT-1: It is one of the most underestimated cameras on this list. Virtually no one knows the brand, that, as mentioned, has produced cameras for all the other brands. It is Japanese quality at its best. CT-1 is a relatively simple camera, that has one huge advantage: It doesn't require a battery to snap images. There is a build-in light meter, that depends on a battery, but if you learn to judge the available light yourself from the so-called "Sunny 16 rule" (we'll get to it later), or do you use a light meter in your mobile phone, the battery is superfluous. The camera shoots purely mechanically on all shutter times from 1 second to 1/1000 second and on B (for longer lasting exposures).

Similar cameras, that does almost the same: *Cosina CT-1G*, *Chinon CE-4* - last mentioned depending on batteries though.

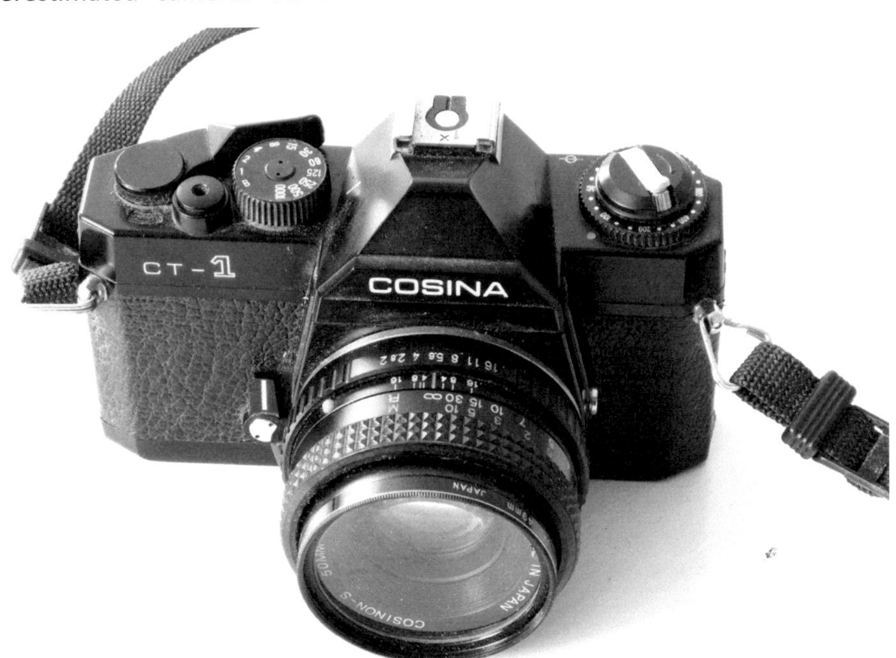

Petri GX-1 Super: What I mentioned on the Cosina CT-1 goes for this camera, that is actually produced by Cosina. The main difference is that the GX-1 goes al the way to 1/2000 second, a huge benefit in bright sunlight.

Pentax MX: A really nice kamera from Pentax with, what I regard as a huge advantage, a mechanical shutter working without batteries. If you have batteries, you also have a light meter. Conversely, like with other mechanical shutters, at the buy you must make sure the longer shutter times work. Set the camera to one second and open the back side, release shutter while looking through the lens. Does it seem like one second? On most older cameras it may be open a bit longer, but now you know and can compensate for it. My MX doesn't work at all at one second, and ½ second is more like one second, but after that it seems to level out. The camera also has a B setting for long exposures, and it has a depth of field button (DOF), so it's possible to judge sharpness levels in front and behind your main motive. We'll discuss this feature later.

Similar cameras, that does almost the same: *Pentax K2* - heavy but sturdy, *Pentax K1000* - delicious, but hyped to high expense, Pentax ME super - fully electronic and only working with batteries, however you can use aperture priority as well as use full manual. Though there is no DOF button.

One important note for all the aforementioned cameras is, that they all use Pentax K lens mount (bayonet), which means that all lenses for Pentax K will fit on the mentioned cameras. And there is a huge selection of lenses available at sensible prices.

Nikon FM2: A real juvel of a camera, with everything that a photographer could want. Shutter with exposures from 1 second to 1/4000 second, an unusually fast shutter for a fully mechanical, DOF button, built-in light meter, Nikons F bayonet with access to a huge selection of lenses produced over a long year span. The camera house is solidly build in metal, actually, the only con is the prices that has risen considerably.

Similar cameras, that does almost the same: *Nikon FM* - the predecessor to FM2, that only has shutter speeds up to 1/1000 second, but otherwise is largely the same.

Minolta X-300: I'm generally not fan of the older cameras from Minolta.

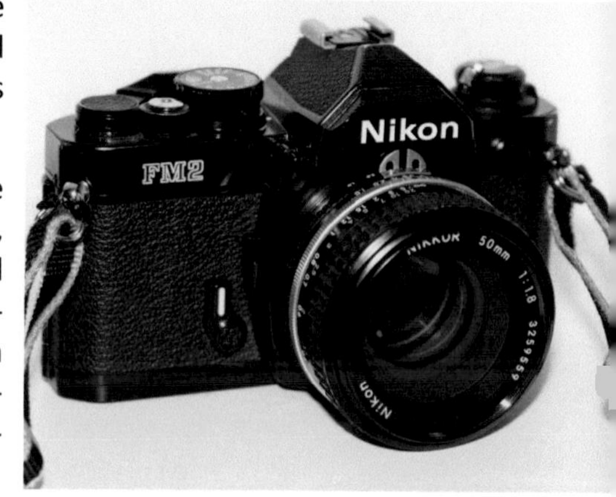

They are great, when they work, and Minolta optics are generally very good, but the electronics are unstable. When I do list one here, the cause is the relatively low price. Additionally, when it works, it contains most of what you need: Aperture priority or manual exposure, light meter, electronic self timer, unfortunately no DOF button and dependence on batteries. Before buying, you should check that the shutter releases, otherwise the capacitors are probably dead, and check that the shutter curtain opens completely. If these thing are not working, it could become an expensive camera. Better go for something else.

Similar cameras, that does almost the same: *Minolta X-500, X-570* both has the weaknesses as the X-300 and are more expensive. The older Minolta SRT cameras are more reliable, has mechanical shutters, and are therefore not battery dependent, but they are heavier and more clumsy.

Konica Autoreflex TC: Konica is probably more known for their point&shoots in fancy colors. Actually, they produced a number of SLRs from which I will highlight the relatively simple Autoreflex TC. It can run without batteries, where you choose both shutter time and aperture, but if you load a battery, you will get the unusual possibility of shutter priority automatic shooting, where the camera sets the aperture. You will be a bit limited in shutter times: 1/8 second to 1/1000 plus B, but as you can get this camera at rather low prices maybe even with the extremely nice 40mm f1.8 lens, this is a very good option.

Olympus OM-10: This is probably one of the most demanded beginners cameras, and for a lot of reasons, but I would question if it´s one of the best. Firstly, you are depending on a battery to shoot, and you can't grow with the camera, as it initially only has aperture priority, and no possibility for manual shooting. You can buy a small device for the camera, thus adding manual mode, but these are not frequently available. Nevertheless, it is a gorgeous camera, easy to use, and if you are using Olympus lenses, you are getting some of the best available. It is often sold with a 50mm f1.8 lens, an awesome lens providing good sharpness and the ability to let the background disappear in a nice soft blur. If the shutter is open on inspection,check that it closes when you insert batteries, otherwise it will probably need an expensive repair.

Olympus OM-40: If you like Olympus cameras and their wonderful lenses, I would suggest that you look towards OM-40, which is marginally more expensive, but gives you three modes: 1). Full automatic, where the camera sets both shutter and aperture. 2). Aperture priority. 3). Last but not least full manual control. Like the OM-10 it has the weakness not to work without batteries. With the added opportunity of full manual, it's a better camera to grow with as a photographer.

Similar cameras, that does almost the same: *Olympus OM1* and *OM2* are more professional Olympus cameras, where OM-1 is fully mechanical, and OM-2 is dependent on batteries. But as prices for both these have sky rocketed, I don't consider them alternatives for the beginner.

Canon AE-1 and *AE-1 Program*: There shall be no doubt, Canon has through the years mad a lot of fantastic cameras, and their lenses can be really nice, even though they have sometimes made some cheap junk. A fully working Canon AE-1/AE-1 Program is a very decent camera, what many buyers have found, unfortunately also resulting in a considerable price rise. You could be lucky to find one at a reasonable price, if you are patient. There is a huge amount of lenses to choose from for the FD mount, that

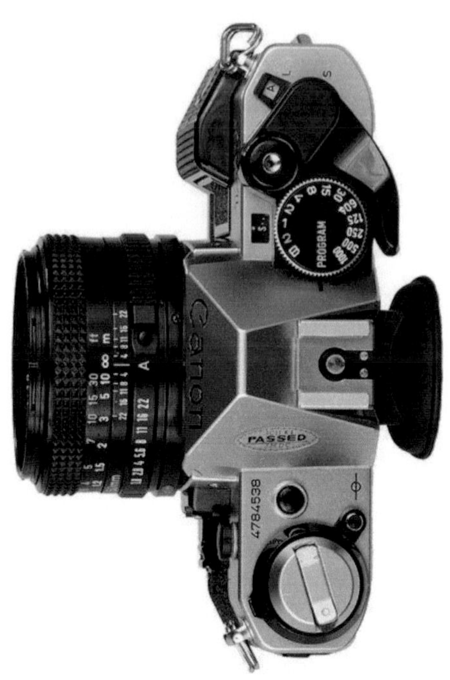

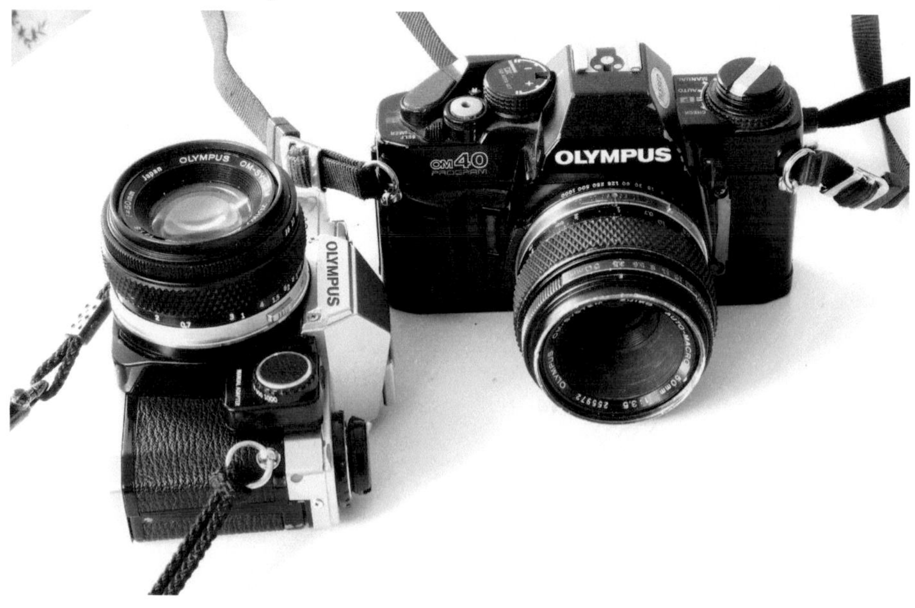

these cameras use, both lenses from Canon, but even from many third party producers like Tokina, Vivitar, Sigma, Tamron among others.

Similar cameras, that does almost the same: *Canon A-1* is seemingly a similar camera, that also have become too expensive, but it is really a delicious camera. A-1 is somewhat more advanced camera that delivers both program mode, shutter priority, aperture priority as well as full manual. There is also a row of fully mechanical models, that are very robust, but weighs a ton.

Canon EOS 500/500n: This is a much more modern camera, that uses another mount then the previous mentioned FD models. It has the EF (Electronic Focus) mount, that Canon has used until they started producing digital mirrorless cameras. One of the advantages of the EOS series of cameras is, that they can use all the EF lenses, Canon has produced since the first EOS camera was introduced in 1987. Furthermore, the third party producers Sigma, Tamron among others have produced lots of lenses for this mount, and some of these for instance Sigmas ART series are high quality products.

EOS 500 is one of the cheapest cameras, you can get. It has aperture and shutter priority, manual control and fully automatic mode. Furthermore, you can use lenses with autofocus, and you can turn this off, if you want full control of focus. The camera has motordrive for advancing and return spooling the film. That means you are totally dependent on the batteries: Two pieces of CR123A battery. The good thing is, that the batteries last very long, usually around 50 films. The EOS 500 is generally very reliable cameras.

Similar cameras, that does almost the same: *Canon EOS 100* er a slightly more advanced camera with shutter times down to 1/4000 second. *Canon EOS 650* was the first camera Canon introduced for the EF mount, and it is almost identical to *EOS 620*, that you should get instead. Both are rock solid cameras. I have used fully functional specimens more than 30 years after their production date.

If you want to get into Nikon land to find something likewise, then *Nikon F301* and *F401* are really nice cameras, but also some of the newer *F50, F65, F70* and especially the semiprofessional *F90X* are really goo choices. F90X was my first more advanced SLR, and I got fantastic images with it. It has shutter times down to 1/8000 second, and a load of other advanced features, but is at the same time very simple to use. The mentioned cameras use Nikons F mount, and there is an equally large selection of lenses as for the Canon EF mount.

Rangefinder

Most people have heard about Leica, famed for their unique quality, but are often blamed for being wildly over-priced. In fact, they are really expensive, some of them exorbitantly so. Nevertheless, that was not the point here, it was just my point that if you know the traditional Lecia, you know what a rangefinder camera is by look at least. In fact, Leica has also produced SLRs, but they are not nearly as known for these as for their rangefinders.

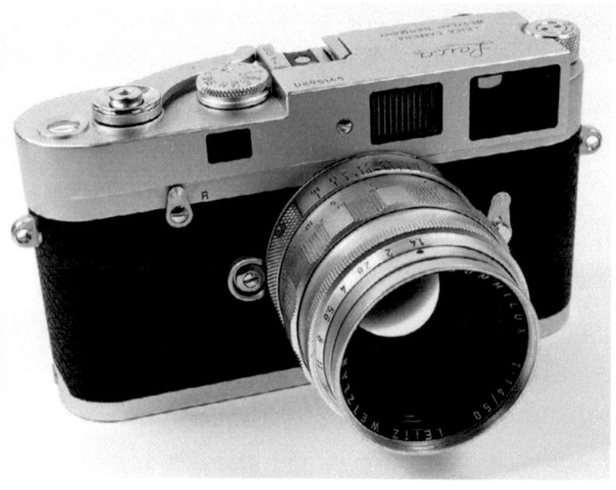

With the rangefinder you don't have the mirror, that makes it possible to view your motive through the lens, that also projects the image on your film. Typically, the rangefinder has the viewfinder in the upper left side of the camera (as you hold the camera), though on some it is placed more centrally, but that doesn't change the principle, and then there is a smaller window more to the left on the camera. The little window projects a small central part of your motive into the viewfinder, and when you set the focus, the position of this projection changes. When the image through the viewfinder and the small projection overlaps, your focus is correctly set. This way this viewfinder measures the distance, and gives name to this type of camera.

On most rangefinders, you cannot change the lens, though the aforementioned Leica cameras has exchangeable lenses, but there is not the same wide choice of lenses, as when you use a SLR camera. There are a few other rangefinders, that give you the same possibility, so Leica is not the only choice, if that is the kind of camera, you would like.

Rangefinder camera examples

Minolta Hi-Matic 7: A relatively boxy, clumsy camera, that in return can give ultra sharp images. The lens is a 45mm, aperture f1.8, that already fully open renders sharp images though maybe except in the extreme corners. But stop down the aperture a bit, and get perfect sharpness. The rangefinder makes sure you can easily focus, and the built-in light meter - though it requires a battery - is fairly precise, furthermore providing both full manual, aperture and shutter priority.

Similar cameras, that does almost the same: *Minolta Hi-Matic 7S, Hi-Matic 9.*

Yashica Minister III: This is a camera based on the old selenium light meter, therefore not requiring a battery. However, it means you must transfer the values to the lens yourself, thereafter choosing your aperture-shutter combination. The rangefinder works nicely securing sharp images.

Konica Auto S2: Again a somewhat large and clumsy camera, that in return has a stellar lens, the Hexanon 45mm f1.8, that is famed for sublime sharpness. Hexanon lenses are generally known to be really excellent lenses. The camera provides full manual or shutter priority, though that requires a battery.

Similar cameras, that does almost the same: *Revue Auto S2* is the same camera, *Konica Auto S3* is a far more compact camera with a highly estimated 38mm f1.8 lens, but this newer model is unfortunately much more expensive. There are several copies of it, but none with the excellent lens.

Olympus 35 RC: Olympus shows once again, how a small camera doesn't need to be functionally limited. The camera has manual mode, shutter priority, and a big, bright viewfinder with information about the shutter time, the camera will select. The only thing that is not so overwhelming is the rangefinder, which is not very clear.

Ricoh 500G/500RF: Yet another small rangefinder, that is sought for both its lens, a 40mm f2.8, and its functionality. You set the shutter time, the camera sets the aperture automatically (with a battery in the camera), or you can choose to set both shutter time and aperture yourself. A small con is, that the rangefinder isn't very precise.

Canon Canonet QL17 GIII: If you want high quality, but don't want Leica prices, and don't need interchangeable lenses, the small robust Canon QL17 GIII is a magnificent offer. The 40mm lens is incredibly sharp, and can create a super nice background separation with its aperture of 1.7. The rangefinder is better than most of the the other small cameras, enabling you to set focus precisely. It has for a long time been my favorite rangefinder, though it's a bit expensive.

Compact camera and point&shoot

Compact cameras are as a type the most variable, and not always that compact. A camera, that resembles a rangefinder camera without the rangefinder, will often qualify as a compact camera. You will have to set the distance yourself, without the help of the rangefinder. Then there are the alternative compact cameras known as "point and shoot" cameras. Here you don't have to do anything except point at your motive and shoot. That is the effect of either fully automatic settings of exposure and focus, or that the camera is so simple there is no settings. The lens could be the so-called fix-focus type, where you can't change focus, easy but at the same time setting up some limitations.

Whereas the compact camera have some possibility of changing settings, the point&shoot has close to none. Nevertheless, some point&shoots have a zoom lens, covering both wide perspectives as well as a binocular like setting.

Compact camera examples

Olympus XA2: This is a crazy compact camera, that in spite of this has a relatively sharp lens. The original XA is a marvelous rangefinder camera, but insanely expensive, and the model I have used only provides focus setting via three symbols for different distances. With its 35mm aperture 3.5 lens the XA2 provides large depth of field, thus the precise focus of the rangefinder isn't necessary. I'll admit that I do like the XA more, just not the insane price.

Olympus Trip 35: This has been a decisive camera for me. It was the first analog camera I used, when returning to analog photography after a few years of digital photography focus. It is a very simpel camera, setting a combination of shutter time and aperture automatically. The only annoying thing is, that it blocks the exposure, if it thinks there is not enough light. Though, there are ways to circumvent this. The lens is very sharp, and the light meter has a selenium cell, not depending on a battery. To celebrate coming back to analog, I bought a

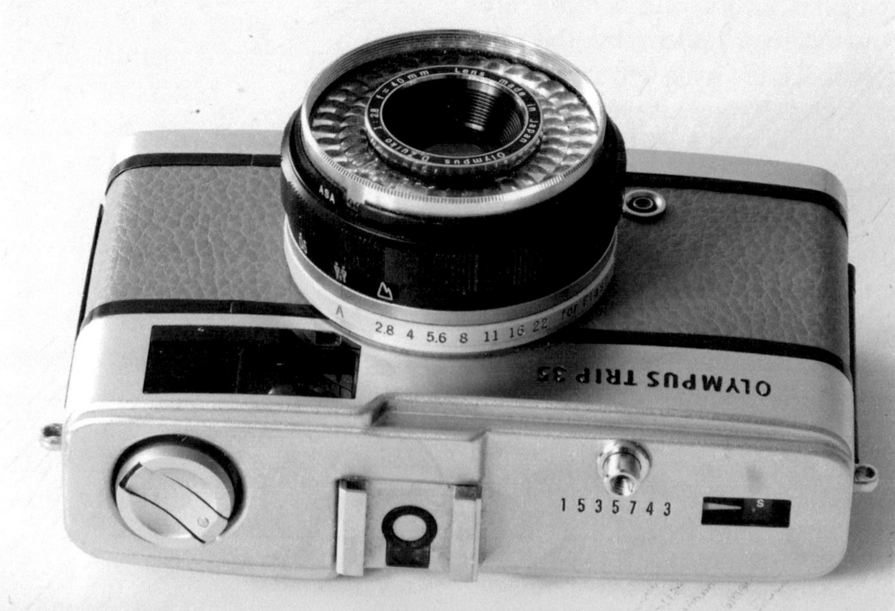

very exotic version of it, dressed in bright leather.

Agfa Optima Sensor: Another camera, that is often available for cheap, but at the same time has sharp optics, is the Agfa Optima Sensor. Especially the models with a Solitar lens are capable of very sharp images. There are also very simple models, and even some with a rangefinder, although these latter are more expensive. All of these cameras have exceptionally nice and bright viewfinders, but the special feature of these cameras are the way you return spool the film. Push a button, and suddenly the film advance lever becomes the return spool lever. Very clever. It has - together with the Olympus Trip 35 - been one of my favorites.

Point&shoot examples

Konica Pop: The original Konica Pop is a very simple but fancy camera coming in a lot of different attention attracting colors, later models are more advanced, some even with a zoom lens. The original has exactly ZERO settings, but is available in black, grey, red, blue, and white, but can even be found in bizarre colors; yellow, bright green, and even pink. The ISO value sets the aperture, there is only one shutter time, focus is fixfocus and hopefully covers the the area, you want to cover. Some believe the name “Pop” came from the colors, but it’s actually the flash, that pops up that has given the name to this camera series. If you need to use the flash, two AA batteries are necessary, otherwise you’ll be fine without batteries.

The lens is a 36mm aperture f4, and if you hit within the range of sharpness provided by the fix-focus the camera actually delivers astonishing results, and it is one of the simplest cameras in use.

Konica Z-Up: The Z-up series of cameras are more advanced, delivering automatic setting, and usually a decent zoom lens. The electronics handles both correctly exposed image, focusing, and motorized film advance. The electronics have been more susceptible to failure over time, thus few cameras have stood the test of time, and works flawlessly today.

I have had a number of different Z-ups, as I was previously sponsored by Konica during my expeditions to the highest mountains in the World. They always delivered nice results. I would highlight *Z-up 110 VP*, that has a lens covering 38-110mm, made all the settings automatically, and provided decently sharp images.

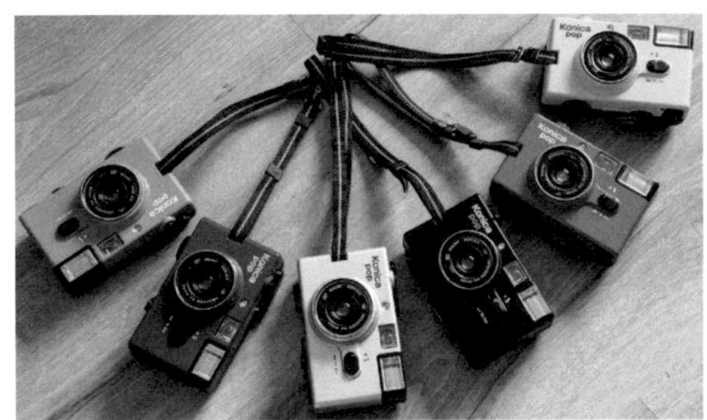

Olympus Mju: This is really a miniature camera, so small that it's incredible there's room for film cassette and the take up spool. The cameras are also available under the name "Stylus," the brand for the Americas. Mju cameras have precise automatic focus and exposure setting. The first cameras has a fixed 35mm f3.5 lens, while later models have zoom lenses, often with a large range. Olympus continued the Mju/Stylus brand into the digital age, therefore it is probably the camera series with the highest sales numbers - that is if you can accept both 35mm analog and digital cameras as one series. Konica Pop competes with this title. My sample of Mju is one of the smallest cameras, I have owned, only my Canon IXUS III APS camera is smaller.

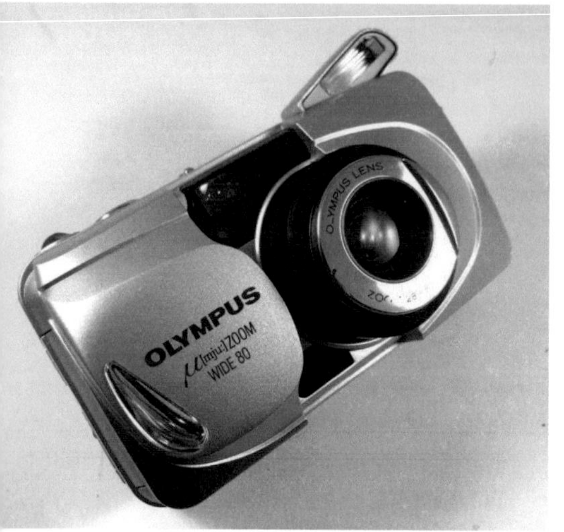

Experimental cameras

I have had many exiting days, and wild expectations, when I got back with exposed film in the cameras I now will describe. With high hopes I developed the film, sometimes to be disappointed, but very often to be amazed by the interesting results. That is the way it works with experimental photography, a little like Forest Gump say it in the movie of the same name (actually, it's his mother who tells him this): "Life is like a box of chocolate, you never know what you get." In my case it is the experimental photography, that can give extraordinary result, or can disappoint unexpectedly.

Maybe you have heard about Holga, or even seen images from it. Some tend to call it a "toy camera," ie something to play with, and not for serious use. It is mainly produced from plastic including the lens. There is no quality control, therefore no two cameras are similar, and will provide the same rendering of a scene. Some cameras deliver decently sharp results, while others have a lot of character ie are unsharp, but can be exploited to provide creative images. That is part of the attraction of the Holga camera. Some will hate it, others will be inspired by the character of the camera to create something unique. There are different kind of Holgas, but most utilize the ones for 120 film, though there are Holgas for 135 film. I will highly

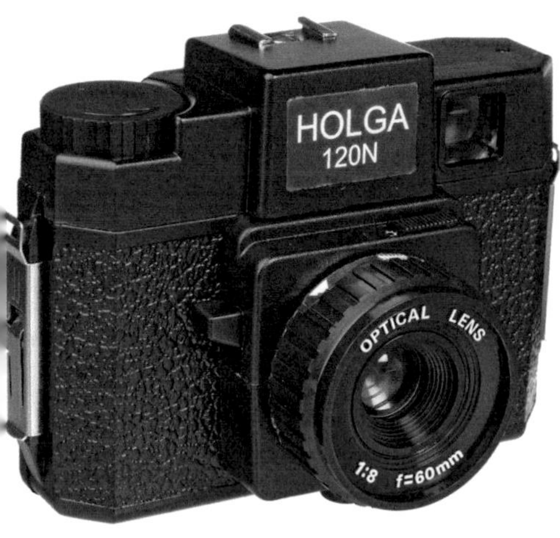

recommend trying this out, once you are beyond the beginner level.

Sprocket Rocket is another toy camera, that also mainly consists of plastic. Contrary to the Holga it only exists for 35mm film. It has to special features, the first of which is revealed in its name. "Sprockets" is another expression for the film advance perforation, and this camera can expose the film almost to the edge, thereby also exposing the sprockets. The other special feature is the image format, not only does it cover almost the entire width of the film, but the length of each frame is 72mm. In other words the total image area is 33mm x 72mm, and thereby a panoramic format. The lens in this is plastic, and just like the Holga, doesn't deliver a completely sharp image except maybe for the center of the image. Furthermore, the frame is not evenly exposed, which is also the case with the Holga. Image borders and extreme corners are darker, something we call vignetting. Nevertheless, it is a fun camera to use, and can provide terrific images - see image next spread.

Another feature shared by Holga and Sprocket Rocket is, that there is no hindrance to make double exposures. In fact you need to be aware of advancing the film, if you want to expose normally. We are on somewhat of a detour, cause it's probably not the cameras you want to begin with, but now you know there is some creative tools awaiting, once you are past learning the basics.

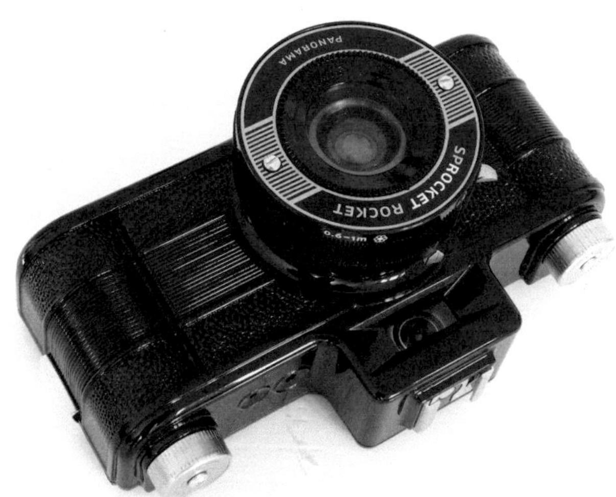

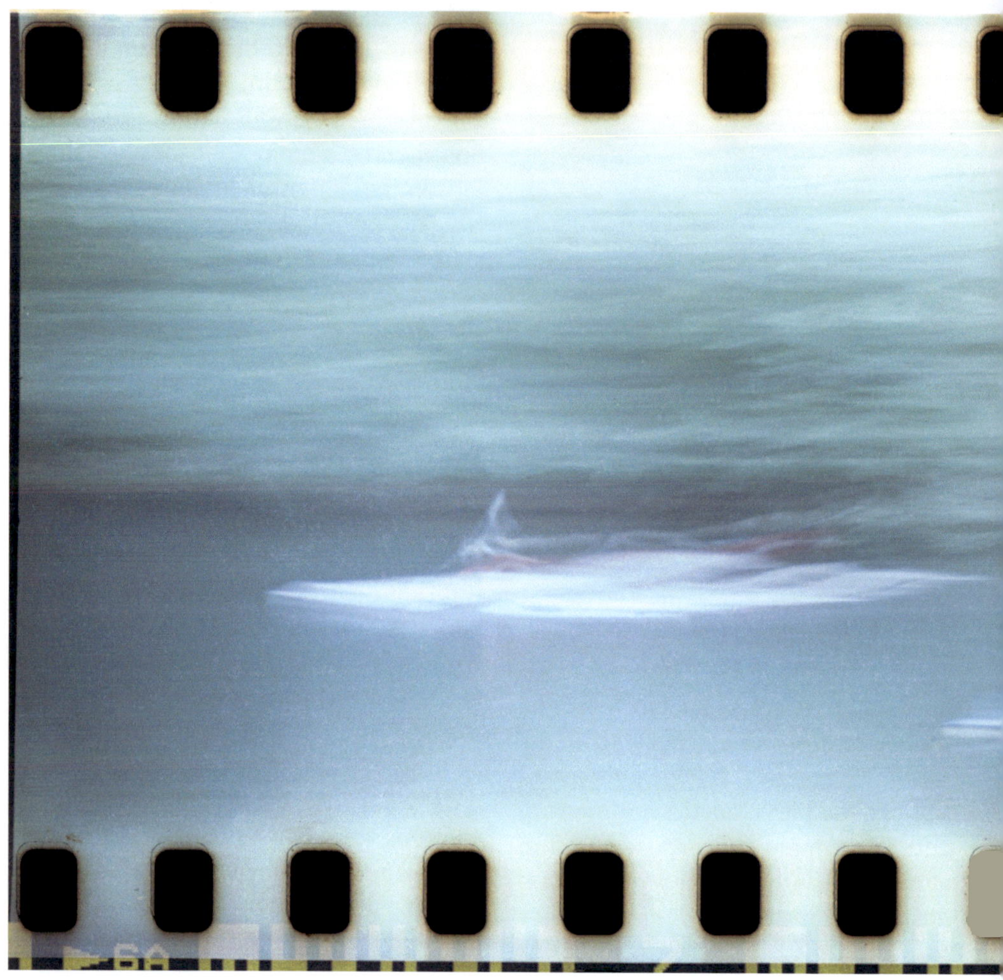

Kayakers on Mølleåen, a small river in my local area.

It is a very dark day with little light on the sky, but I decide to be creative, and I take my most toy like camera and walk into nature to find some inspiration. While walking along a river I see three kayakers coming towards me.

I set my Sprocket Rocket camera on the B setting, where I can keep the shutter open as long as I keep the shutter button pressed, I set the aperture to the smallest size, not allowing much light to enter into the film chamber. That results in a fairly long exposure in order to create an image on the film, and therefore I expect to see a movement blur.

As the kayakers are just in front of me, I press the shutter, pans following the kayakers on their passing. I have the shutter open around a second before releasing the shutter, just hoping for a nice result.

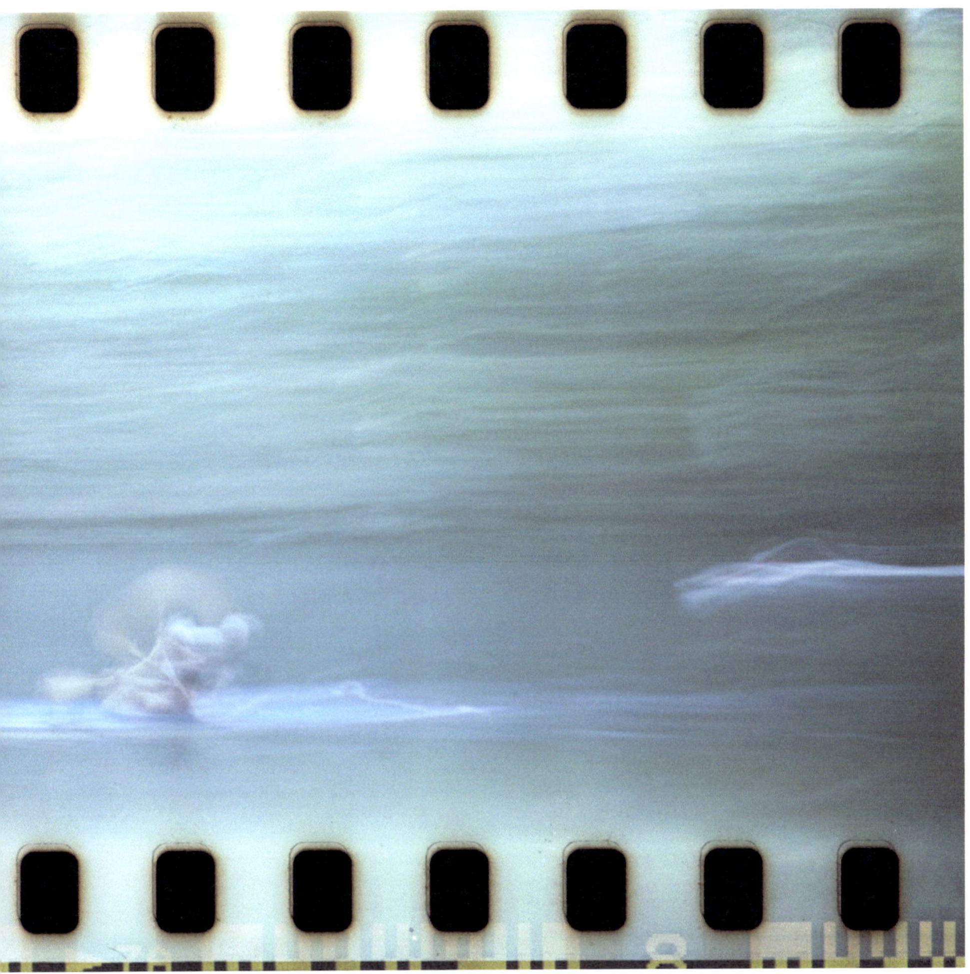

After shooting a load of other images, I arrive home. I rewind the film, and get it out of the camera and put it into a developing tank. I make my color developer, the socalled C41 used for color negative film, ready. It is not an easy developing process, as it requires strict temperature control and exact timing of the development.

As the results emerge from the developing tank after around half an hour, I'm very pleased. The image of the rowers are exactly as I had visualized it. Lots of movement blur, but still recognizable subjects, and you can even see the movement of the kayakers. Furthermore, the colors of the water and the trees around the river merge in a very beautiful way. I'm not always very fond of the sprockets in film, that are exposed in this camera, sometimes it disturbes, but to me and in this image it adds an element, like an abstract tact for the rowers.

Overall it is one of the creative images, I am most proud of.

Readying your camera

When readying you camera for use, there's a number of things you need to do. What and how depends a lot on your specific camera. To your advantage, you should find the manual for your camera on the internet. Search for the name of your camera, and the word "manual," and you will usually find it as a PDF ready to download.

Battery

Do your camera need a battery? Even if it can hold a battery, it is a previously described not necessarily a must. It depends on the shutter, as many older camera, as we have seen, has mechanical shutter. But if you want the light meter to work, you might need a battery. Probably you'll think, "but how shall I manage without an exposure measurement." It is a good question, but there are ways to manage without a light meter, and judge the exposure yourself, and there are exposure apps for both Android and iPhone. Of course you can just decide to put batteries in the camera, and rely on the built in light meter, if your camera has one. Examples on this camera type are the magnificent Petri GX-1 Super, that has mechanical shutter up to 1/2000 second, but only need the battery to drive the light meter. That is a kind of camera that I prefer for expeditions to the mountains, where the low temperatures can make the battery unusable. With the mechanical shutter I can always shoot, if I can judge the light myself.

You already heard about the selenium cell based light meget, that doesn't require a battery. The selenium cell creates power when hit by the light, driving the meter needle. On older cameras, like the aforementioned Yashica Minister, this value is read and transferred manually, by you, to the lens. The value is the so-called EV value, and from that you can then choose a combination of shutter time and aperture, that will give a correct exposure of the film. Another example

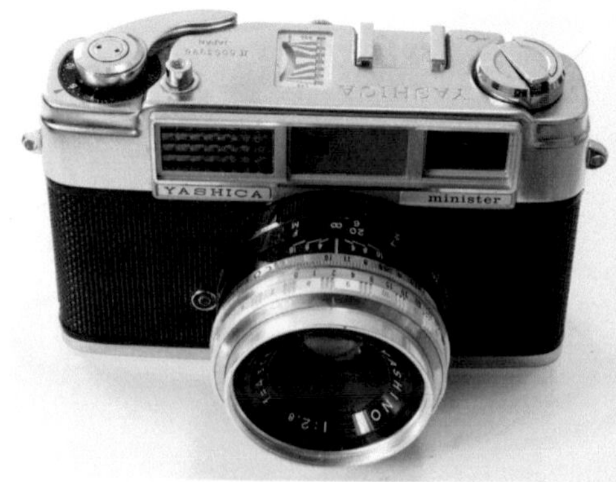

of the selenium cell is the Olympus Trip 35, that automatically chooses a shutter time and aperture setting - see the image on page 30.

On newer cameras the battery is far more important, as not only their light meter, but also shutter and for some even film advance is depending on electronics. Naturally, the electronics need power to work, and many of these cameras lock up if the battery lacks or fails. An example, you have heard of, is the popular Olympus OM-10, that uses to small button cell batteries. If you fire the shutter without the batteries, the mirror will lock up as it does during normal exposure, but it will stay there, and the shutter will not fire. Following this the camera will be locked, you cannot advance the film, and the viewfinder will be black. Once you insert batteries the shutter will fire, and the mirror return, after which you can advance the film.

Another example is the Nikon F-301 and several other cameras in the same series, that uses 2 to 8 pieces of double A or triple A batteries. The reason for these larger batteries are, that the film advance and return spooling is motorized, and that requires far more power than button cells can provide.

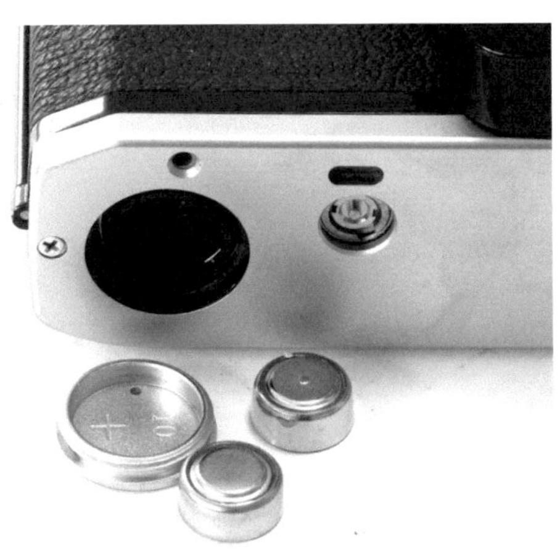

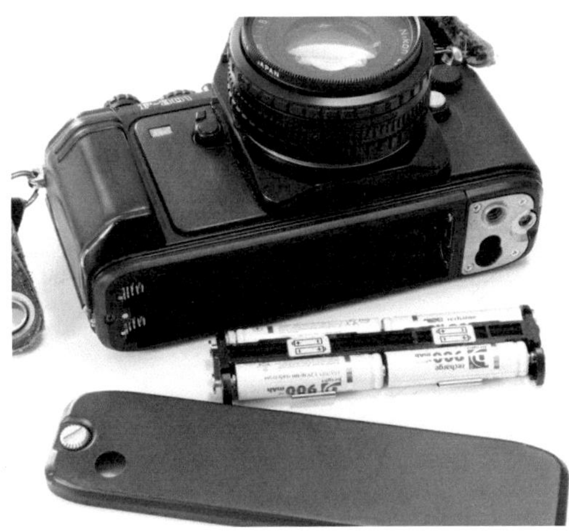

Mounting the lens

If you have a rangefinder camera, a compact camera, or a point&shoot, you probably don't have interchangeable lenses, that means you are all ready. Though, you have to be careful when shooting, as you need to be aware of the lens cap. You can look through the viewfinder, and not see that the lens cap is blocking the lens. As we have seen some rangefinders have a light meter around the lens, that might make you aware of the lens cap.

The popular Olympus Trip 35 will block your shooting, unless enough light hits the meter. Unfortunately, on this exact camera, the blocking feature often ceases to work. You have to experiment with your own camera, to explore if it in any way makes you aware of the forgotten lens cap. I must admit, once in a while to have forgotten the lens cap, fortunately, quickly realising the mistake. I can't recall having missed a dream motive because of a forgotten lens cap, but it could happen.

If you have a SLR camera, and there is not lens mounted, you need to do that. All cameras I know of have an index on both the camera and the lens. Theses two needs to be aligned in order to insert the lens into the mount.

On most cameras, you then turn the lens clockwise until it clicks to its locking position. Nikon chose to do it the opposite way with their F-mount, where you turn the lens counterclockwise. On the older Canon cameras that use the FD mount, the earliest lenses has a small locking ring, that need to be turned clockwise instead of turning the whole lens.

It is a bit different, if you have one of the even older cameras, that uses the

Mounting a lens on a Canon with the EF bayonet.

The two rings shows the markings on respecitively the camera and the lens. They need to be aligned for the lens to get into the mount. Finally, the lens is turned clockwise until it clicks into place.

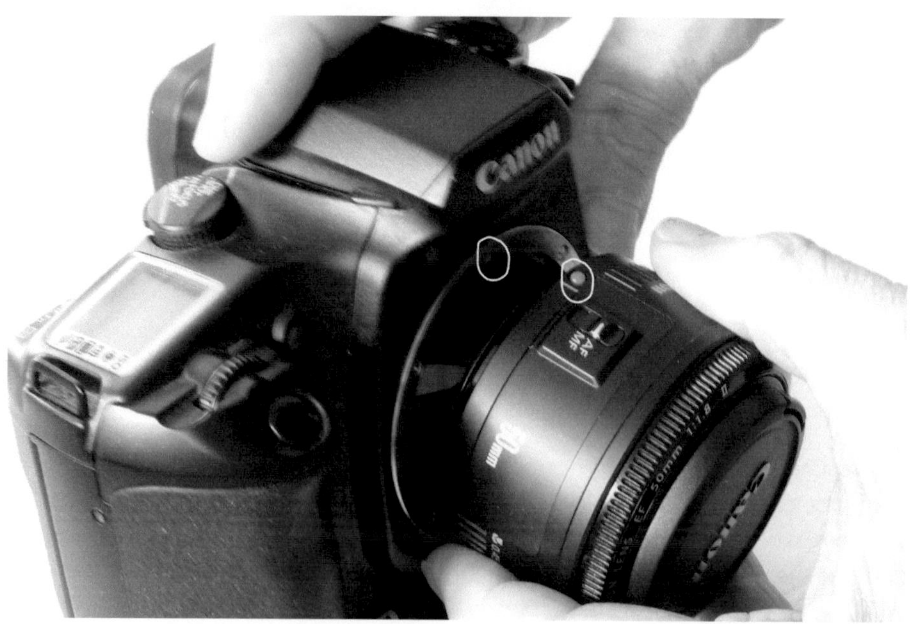

so-called M42 mount. It is a screw mount with a diameter of 42mm, and the lens simply has to be screwed into the mount until it is firmly mounted. In fact, there are other screw mounts, but they are rare and work the same way as the M42 mount.

The point of this section is, when buying a new lens, you just have to be aware of what mount your camera has in order to get a fitting lens. A few adaptable lenses have been made, that could be made to fit almost any camera mount eg. Tamron adaptall.

With lens mounted, I suppose you now have a camera ready with a lens mounted.

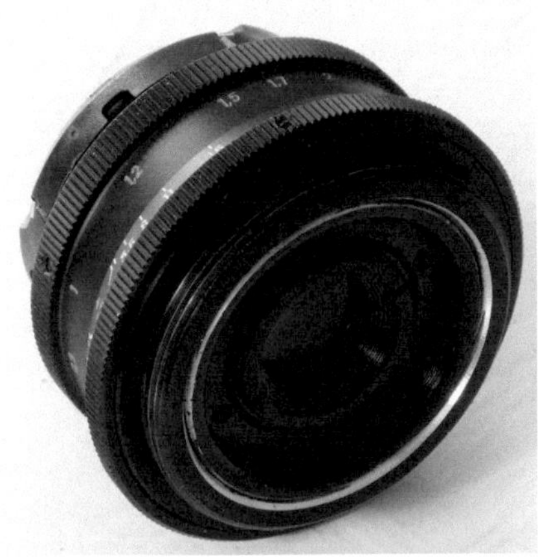

On of the oldest mounts for interchangeable lenses are of the screw type, that means there is a thread on the lens that fits into a corresponding thread on the camera hous. The image shows a lens with the widely used M42 mount.

Inserting your film

Now you need to have the camera opened, and make the film ready.

There are several different locking mechanisms for the back of the camera, you need to realize which one applies to your camera.

Some cameras are opened by a mechanism on the left side of the camera, that goes for most Canon EOS and Nikons F cameras.

Others are opened by a small lever on the underside of the camera house. That goes for Yashica Minister for instance.

Yet others are opened on the right side of the camera house, for instance Agfa Optima Sensor.

The opening on a Agfa Optima Sensor camera is served by a small lever on the right side of the house. Other cameras has a lever either on the left side or a few has it on the underside of the camera house.

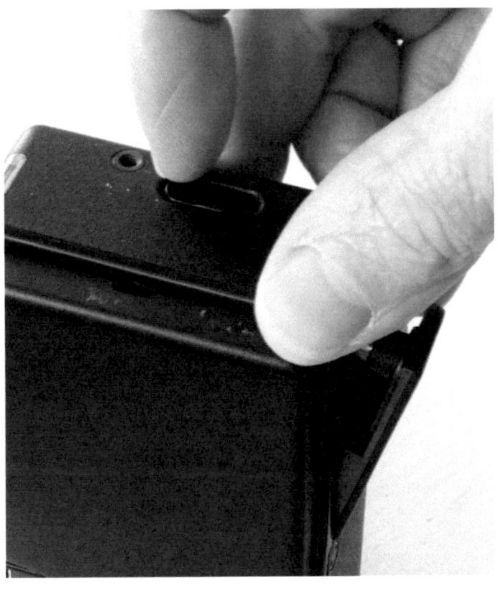

By far the predominant part of analog cameras are opened by pulling op in the return spool lever on the left side of the camera. That goes for almost all the older Canon FD cameras, Nikons earliest cameras including the first in the F series, the X series from Minolta, the M series from Pentax, the OM series from Olympus, and a lot of other cameras.

Then you pull a bit of film out of the cassette, just enough to reach the uptake spool on the other side of the camera, and enough to fasten it to the spool. Usually, there is a slot, that the film is inserted into, and sometimes there is a small protrusion that needs to catch the film perforation.

When you think the film sits cor-

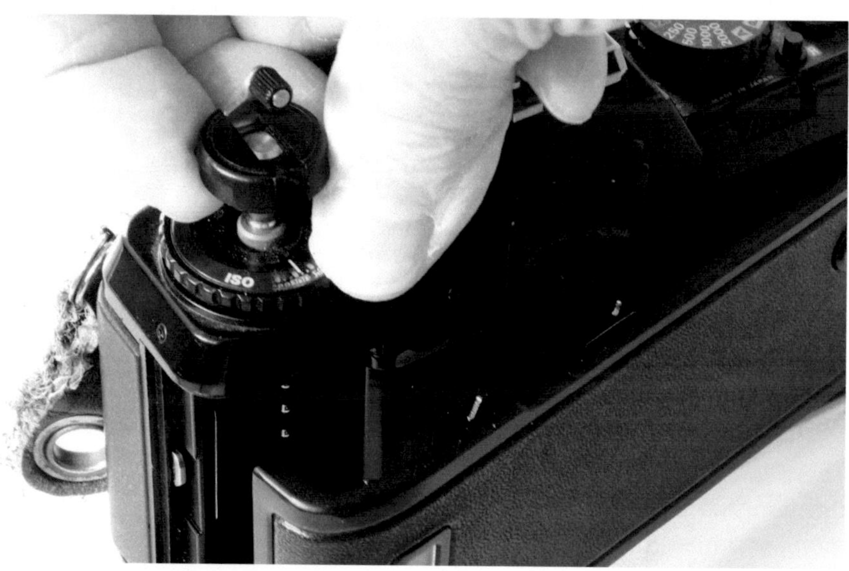

Presuming, you now have the camera open, the film has to be inserted correctly. Again there are several different ways depending on camera type, and if it is a motorized camera.

Lets go with the manual cameras first. Normally, the film is inserted in a depression on the left side, but the aforementioned Agfa Optima Sensor has the depression on the right side.

rectly, you advance the film a single frame while the camera is still open. You are not loosing this frame, as the film is numbered with this in consideration. It is important to assure the film is being advanced correctly, and it doesn't slip the uptake spool. When you are sure everything works perfectly, you can close the back side of the camera. Be sure it closes firmly with an audible click.

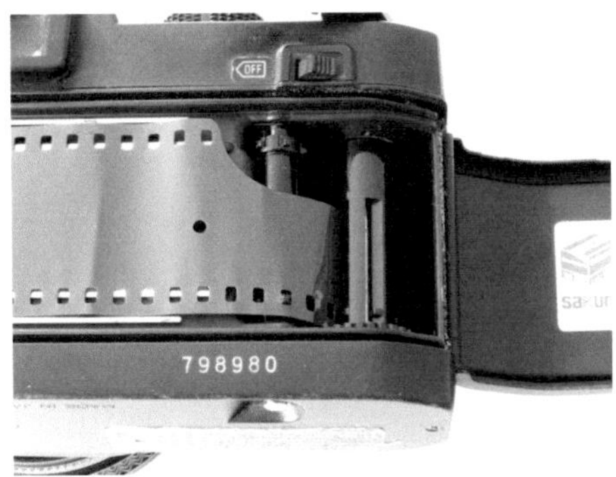

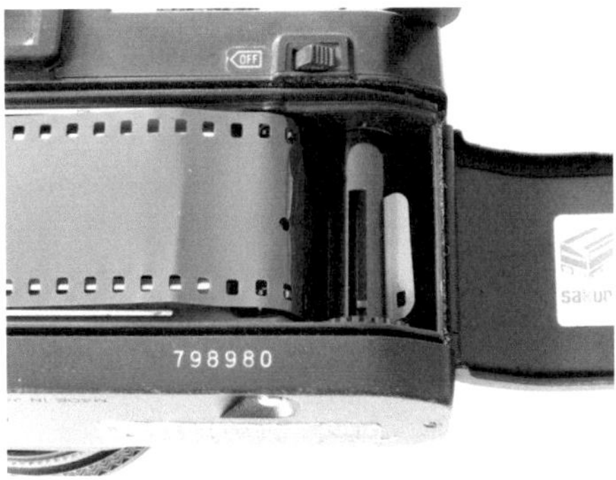

If your camera has motorized film advance it is just as important, that the film is positioned correctly.

A few of the Canon EOS models are sensitive, and if you pull to much film out of the cassette, they can't get grip of the film. Usually, on this type of camera there is an indicator, eg a red marking or arrow, that indicates where the end of the film shall be positioned, when you close the camera. Some cameras immediately advance the film, when you close the back, while others do this when you power them up, or when you press the shutter button.

Cameras with motorized film advance often have very easy film insertion.

Nevertheless, you have to be careful whereto you put the tip of the film. Some cameras are sensitive to correct placement, like to the marking by my thumb. Otherwise the film wont advance.

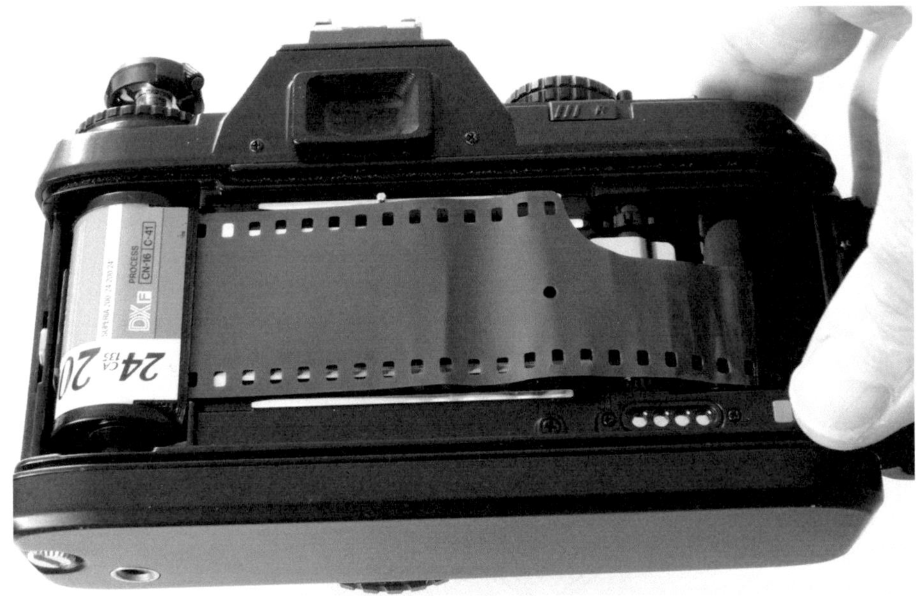

Setting film sensitivity

If you have a 100% manual camera without any kind of light meter, you can skip this section, as you don't need to set the film sensitivity on your camera. Though, in case you have a separate light meter, or use an app on your mobile phone, you might to enter the film sensitivity there. Unfortunately, I can only help by telling you to read the ISO setting from the film into your measuring device.

Newer analog cameras with electronics usually read the film sensitivity from the film cassette. If you are using older, expired film or you have loaded cassettes from larger rolls of raw film, there's probably no DX coding on the cassette - or worst case wrong coding. You will need to read on about how to set the ISO value yourself.

There is a lot of different ways to set the ISO, and we'll cover the most common types from of the previously described cameras.

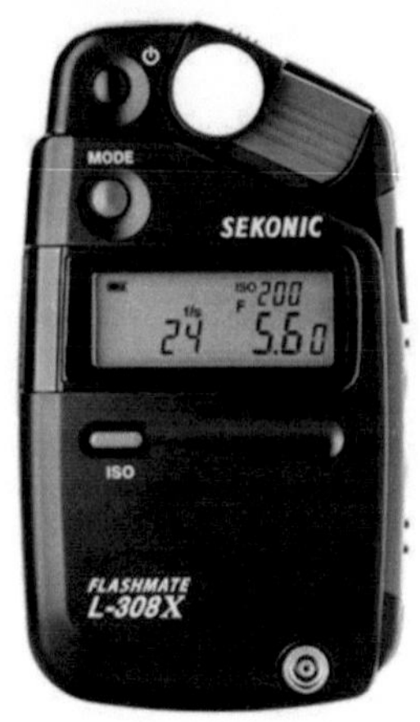

For a serious analog photographer, a light meter is a must, as it make it possible to measure light in difficult conditions, where you might not rely entirely on your cameras built in light meter.

If you have completely manual camera, the light meter also becomes a necessity.

Below to the left in the film chamber, you see the contacts, that reads the DX coding/ISO value for the inserted film.

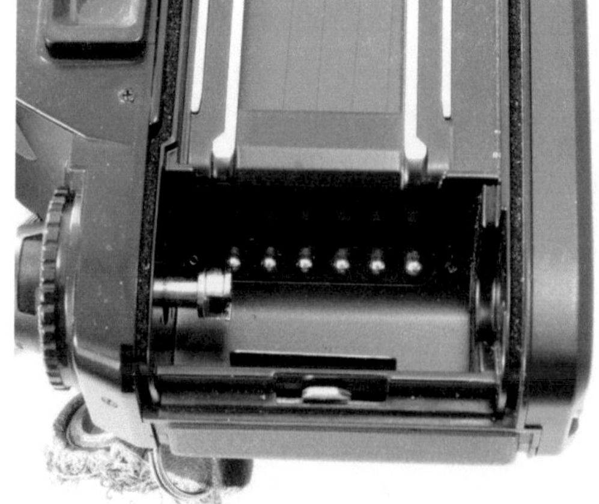

Below to the right, you see an example of the DX coding on the film casette. It is the shiny fields on the casette, that transfers the sensitivity.

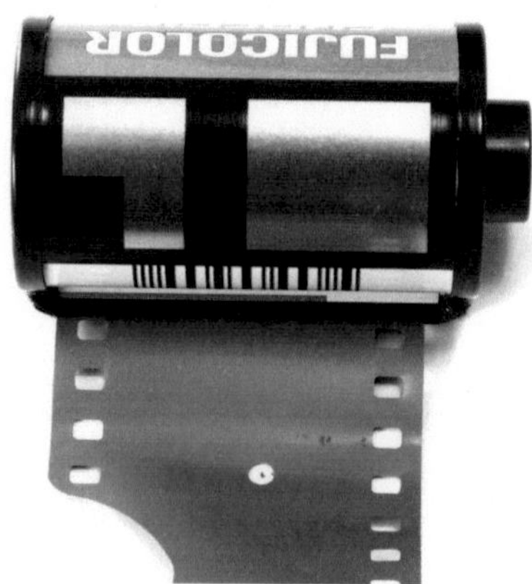

Olympus Trip 35 is a good example on how to set sensitivity on early cameras with a selenium light meter around the lens. On this camera the outhermost ring around the lens is turned to set the sensitivity. A lot of cameras from the same period has the ring placed on the front of the lens around the outhermost lens element, that goes for the Ricoh 500 series and many Minolta rangefinder cameras.

Many older SLRs like Pentax MX, Konica Autoreflex TC, and Canon F-1 has a ring inside the shutter selection dial. Usually you lift the dial in order to be able to turn it. The value visible in the cut-out is the ISO value you have set.

Other older SLRs have an ISO ring in the other side of the camera house beneath the return spool lever. That goes for the Minolta X series, Pentax ME series, and the Canon A-1.

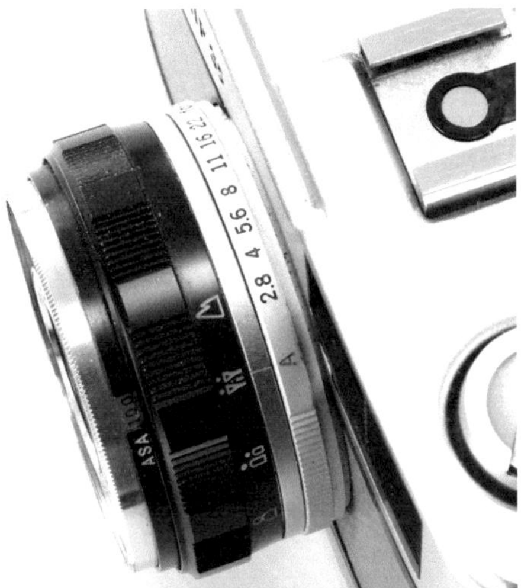

The film sensitivity setting on the outher ring of the lens of an Olympus Trip 35 - here named with the older ASA designation.

On many older cameras like the Olympus the sensitivity settings only range from 25-400, while newer cameras often go all the way to ISO 3200.

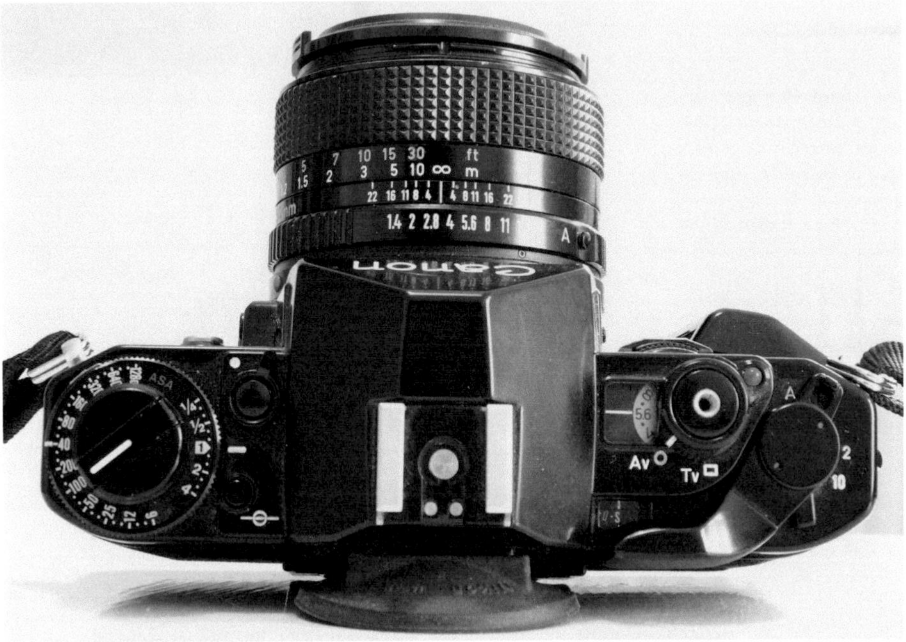

If none of the above procedures doesn't apply to your camera, you will have to search for a place where values like for instance 25, 50, 100, 200, 400, 800. On some cameras you'll note two further values apart from the aforementioned, for instance between 100 and 200 the values 125 and 160. There are film with sensivity in-between the former values, which are considered the ordinary values, where each step represents a doubling of the sensitivity. Both Ilford and Kodak have produced film with ISO 80 sensitivity, which is 1/3 below ISO 100 in sensitivity. If you don't have the "lesser" values, you can set the sensitivity to the nearest number. Film is rather robust especially with regard to a bit of overexposure, though not as happy to be underexposed.

Hopefully, you have now found a way to set the sensitivity on your camera, in order to enable any kind of light meter or automatic exposure setting.

Climbing in Wilde Kaiser in the northern part of the Alps.

The extreme contrast in the bright light in the mountains often challenge digital cameras. Black & white film has a relatively large latitude, and it is often possible to show details in both highlights and in darker parts of the image.

To me, the way the elements of nature like rocks and clouds are reproduced in the analog image is an important part. It adds to a more natural look as compared to the more clinical look of digital images.

Especially, when I consider my older images like this from 1984, then the historical element of the image is reinforced by the analog look. Therefore, I believe that in some years the value of the analog images I make these days will increase for me - more so than the digital images.

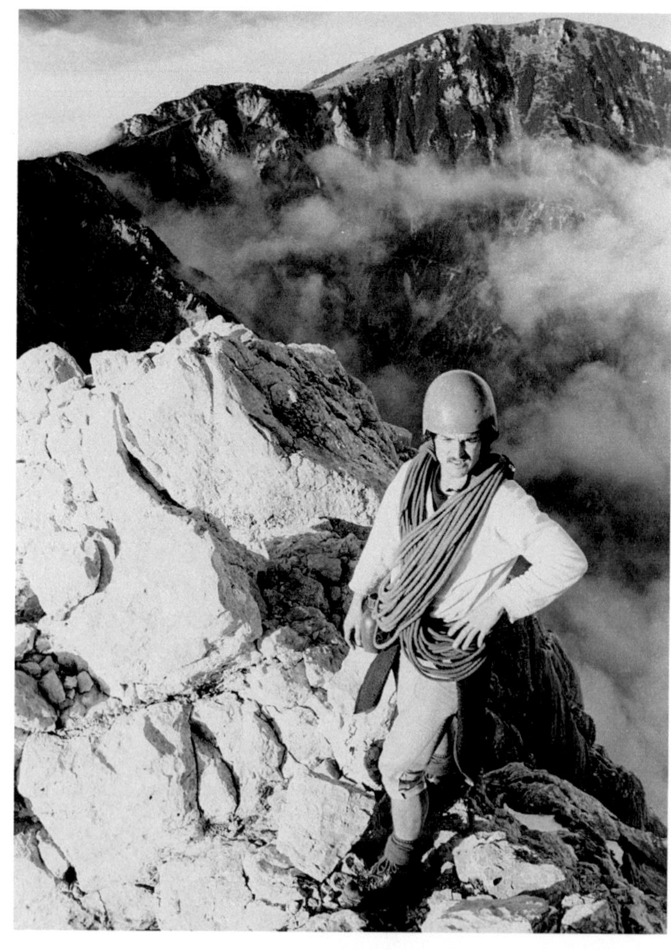

Basisc technique

How to get correctly exposed images

The exposure triangle

There are three parameters, that together decide whether the image is correctly exposed. As photographers we talk about "the exposure triangle." If you change one of the parameters it has influence on the others. The three parameters are:

The fvilm sensitivity, that we have already discussed.

The shutter time. The longer the shutter is open, the more light hits the film.

The aperture of the lens. The more open the aperture, the more light hits the film.

However important a correct exposure is, all three parameters has other effects, that are important to understand to become more creative with your photography.

As we've seen the film sensitivity will influence the grain structure in the film and the contrast, ie the difference between bright and dark.

Shutter time

The shutter time, which on typical cameras is between 1 second and 1/1000 second, has, apart from the amount of light that hits the film, also influence on the sharpness in the image. If you photograph a fast moving object, you won't be able to freeze the movement, unless you use a short shutter time.

No matter how steady your hand is, a very long shutter time will lead to a shaken camera, and thus an uns-

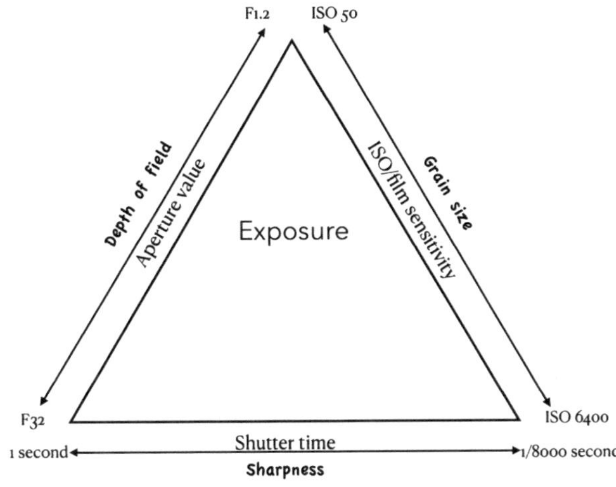

The principle of the exposure triangle is, that you can place your exposure in the triangle depending on the measured values.

Following that, you will be able to see, how the other values change if you change one of the parameters: ISO, aperture value, and shutter time.

In praxis the exposure triangle is not used for anything else than illustrating how the three parameters are correlated.

harp image. At what shutter time you can hand hold your camera without camera shake depends, apart from how steady you hand is, on the focal length of the lens. A telephoto lens, that works like a pair of binoculars, will require a short to very short shutter time.

The rule of thumb is, that you can get sharp images, if the shutter time is at least 1/lens focal length in millimeters. For instance, if you have a 200mm lens, then the shutter time needs to be 1/250 second or even faster (there is no 1/200 on the camera). On the other hand, if you work with a 24mm wideangle, you can use a long shutter time of 1/30 second (again there is no 1/25).

Focal length

If you use a SLR of newer date, some of the available lease has image stabilization - by Canon named OIS (Optical Image Stabilization) and by Nikon VC (Vibration Reduction). This feature enables the use of longer shutter time than elsewise. I have been able to obtain sharp images on my 600mm telephoto lens at 1/125 second. That is three exposure values (so-called stops) slower (1/1000 > 1/500 > 1/250 > 1/125 second) than normally hand holding your camera. Nonetheless, I will recommend a tripod, if you often use this kind of powerful telephoto lenses.

You can also exploit movement and following unsharpness for creative purposes. For instance if you follow a bicyclist passing by, shooting on a long shutter time, the cyclist could at best be perfectly sharp, while the background will be blurred in a way that indicates movement. For creativity, experimenting with shutter time can be really rewarding.

Often it is said, that for an image to be perfect, it must be sharp. I'm definitely opposing this view. Many of my own images, that I'm most proud of, are actually consciously shot unsharp either because of movement or because I chose not to set the focus correctly. Used creatively unsharpness can create art, as opposed to a perfectly sharp image of the same motive, that rather could be consi-

Focal length	Shutter time	Shutter time (steady hand)	Lens with OIS of 3 stops
28 mm	<1/30 second	1/15 second	1/4 second
50 mm	<1/60 second	1/30 second	1/8 second
85 mm	<1/125 second	1/60 second	1/15 second
200 mm	<1/250 second	1/125 second	1/30 second
300 mm	<1/500 second	1/250 second	1/60 second
500 mm	<1/500 second	1/500 second	1/60 second

dered documentation. Have another look at my image of the kayak rowers, shot on a shutter time of 1 second on my Sprocket Rocket experimental (toy?) camera.

Aperture

We have arrived at the rather confusing subject of aperture. Why is a small value equal to a large opening, and a high value is a small opening?

When we consider the F-stop of the lens, it is a fraction that is calculated as follows:

The focal length in millimeters divided by the size of the aperture in millimeters

Coming from Focal length, this fraction is named F-stop. But lets consider some examples to make it easier.

A 50mm lens with a largest aperture of 25mm will have an F value of 50/25 = 2, which is named F2. It doesn't mean that this is the only aperture, as the aperture can be closed. If we assume the smallest aperture is at 3mm, the aperture value will be 50/3 = app. 16. For this lens the aperture scale would look like this:

2 – 2,8 – 4 – 5,6 – 8 – 11 – 16

It is important to note that each of these steps represent a 50% reduction in the amount of light passing the lens.

Lets go with a telephoto lens as well. In order to have an aperture of F2, a moderately powerful lens of 300mm would need an opening of 150mm. That lens would become excessively large and unwieldy to carry around, and would become extremely expensive with the huge amount of high quality glass necessary. Thus no such lens is on the market. For the more manageable 300mm lens, the largest aperture could be around 75mm, which would result in an F-stop 300/75 or F4. Somewhat larger apertures exist in 300mm lenses, but due to an extreme price, they are for the professional photographer only.

Additionally, note that the aperture of the lens does a lot more than decide the amount of light hitting the film, we'll get to that in the next section.

The connection between F stops and shutter time.

I suppose you have already noted, there is a connection between the aperture values and the shutter time. Every shutter time faster corresponds to halving the amount of light, for instance when going from 1/60 second to 1/125, as the shutter is open half the time. As described a full aperture value also corresponds to halving or doubling the amount of light - depending on which way on the scale, we are moving. Then there most be combinations, that result in the same amount of light to the film. Let's go with an example.

If we say, your light meter tells you, the correct exposure will be 1/125 second and F8. Then by moving one step on each of the scales, but in different directions, you can make sure the same amount of light reaches the film. All combinations in the table will result in the same exposure.

Shutter time	1/30 sec.	1/60 sec.	1/125	1/250	1/500	1/1000
Aperture	16	11	8	5.6	4	2.8

Note that the scale "jumps" a bit from 1/60 to 1/125 to have "nice" values, when we go higher; 1/250, 1/500, 1/1000, 1/2000, 1/4000, 1/8000 and so forth. By the way, a shutter time of 1/8000 is almost only possible in professional cameras. Some, even in the non-expensive end, deliver 1/4000 second, but most older cameras top out already at 1/500 or 1/1000.

Sunny-16 rule

A marvelous and simple rule exists, that is used to judge the exposure settings on your camera, and works in most situations. The rule is named "the Sunny-16 rule," and you might think, why exactly. It makes sense, when I explain it.

Use your camera on a bright sunny day, set the aperture to 16, then choose your shutter time to 1 over the ISO value of your film. An example: Lets say, on this bright sunny day, you have chosen an ISO 100 film, you set the aperture to 16, and then you choose 1/100 second. That is not possible, but the value that come closest is 1/125, and that's just fine.

You might feel a little restrained, but think about what we just went through, the dependence between shutter time and aperture. So now it's easy to find a better combination for what you want to photograph.

An example: Lets say, you want to make a portrait, and want a blurred background. Then you would want a low aperture value (we'll come to the subject of depth of field in next section, for now just believe what I'm saying). You choose aperture 4, and the calculation would then tell you to use a shutter time of 1/2000 second, for the same exposure to happen. If your camera has that shutter time, everything is fine, if it doesn't, you must find the combination, that come closest to what you want. Alternatively, you may move your subject to a place out of direct sun, maybe in the shadow of a tree.

Obviously, you don't always shoot under a bright sun, but there is also advice for that, with the starting points in the opposite table.

You have now been through most of the basics, and you will be able to achieve decent results every time.

The next sections will help you become more creative. You can read them later, if for now you just want to get going.

In shadow and at sunset	Aperture 4
Strongly overcast (no shadows seen)	Aperture 5.6
Overcast (almost no shadows visible)	Aperture 8
Slightly overcast (soft shadows visible)	Aperture 11
Blue sky (harsh shadows)	Aperture 16
Beach or snow under a blue sky	Aperture 22

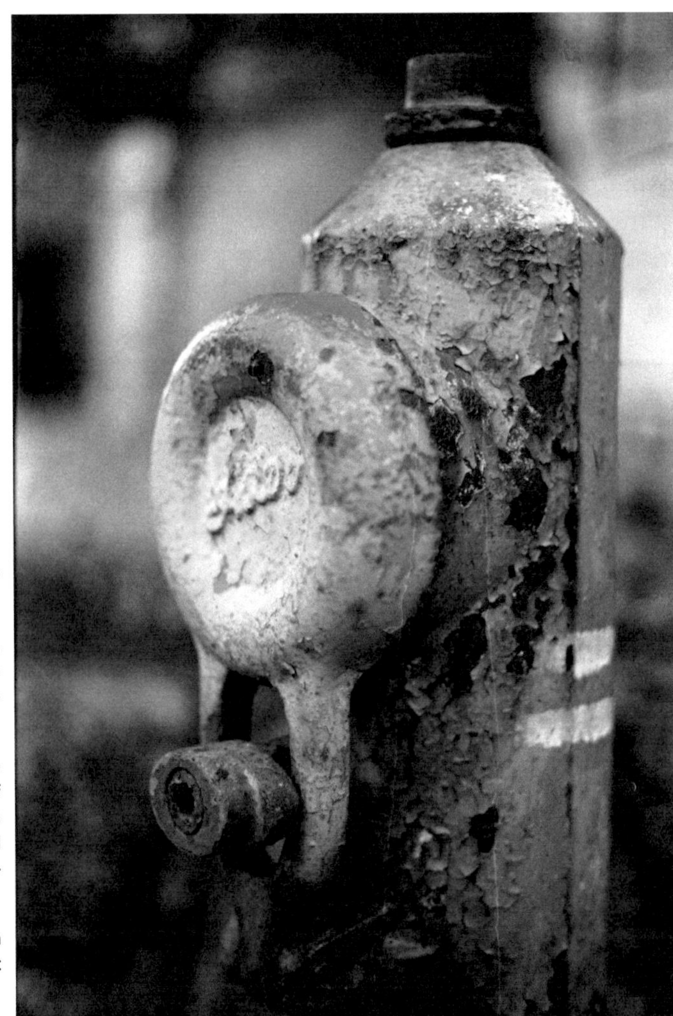

An image of an old rusty fire hydrant.

Many details are visible, but especially the delicious film look adds a pleasing aesthetic.

I don't think the image would be as expressive if it was shot to perfection on a super modern digital camera with high resolution.

Olympus OM40 with a 50mm f1.8 lens shot at f2.8.

More advanced techniques

Take control of the depth of field

One of the deciding factors of how your image will look is the depth of field.

Let's take two examples, that I will exploit further, when get to the sections on different shooting scenarios. We'll take the short version here.

In the first situation you are in the nature, and you would like most of the image, foreground as well as background, to become sharp. In this case you will choose a high aperture value for instance f11 or even higher. That insures a large depth of field. If you have a camera with DOF (Depth of Field) button, you can press this after setting the aperture. Your viewfinder will become darker, but at the same time, you can judge how much of your motive renders sharply. But it is a bit difficult at very high apertures, as the viewfinder becomes very dark. Although we can conclude, large aperture value = large depth of field, the distance to the motive also plays a major role. Close objects result in smaller depth of field.

The other situation is, that you want to photograph a smaller object or maybe a portrait, and you want the object/person to stand out from the background, and disturbing objects in the foreground. One way to obtain this isolation is by using a small depth of field, so small that only your motive is sharp, while the rest of the image is blurred, this way the background seems distant and doesn't disturb.

On the subject of background blur, there is a quite a discussion going on, as some lenses have been extremely hyped for their ability to create a very distinct unsharp zone around the motive. The internet has gone crazy about these special lenses abilities. Some photographers that buy into this can almost spend all their money on lenses in order to pursue this image look. Anyway, there are some pretty cheap russian Helios lenses, that can create these wonderful results. You can find examples on this on my homepage www.K2-photography.dk in the section on vintage lens tests. The images are shot on digital cameras, but that doesn't change the abilities of the lenses with regard to background blur, and you can achieve exactly the same effect with a film based camera.

Apart from what is mentioned in the image caption, you can learn another lesson: When you stop down the aperture a lot, I used f22 in the example with the led lights, then shining objects will be rendered with a star like effect. You can exploit this

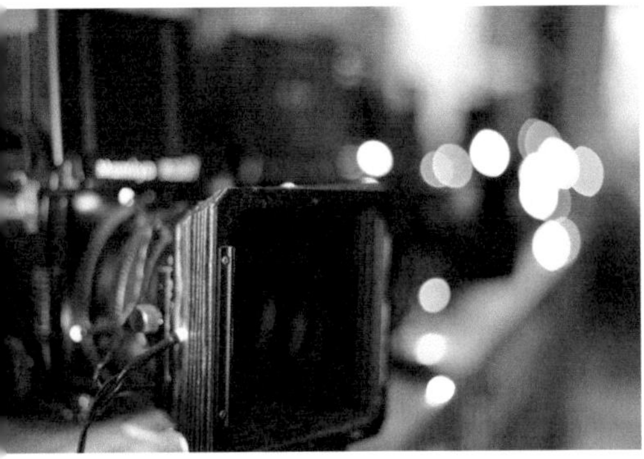

One of my camera display shelfs illuminated by led lights at Christmas is there to visualize how depth of field increases by use of increasingly higher aperture values. The image series is shot with a Canon 50mm lens with aperture values from f1.8 to 22.

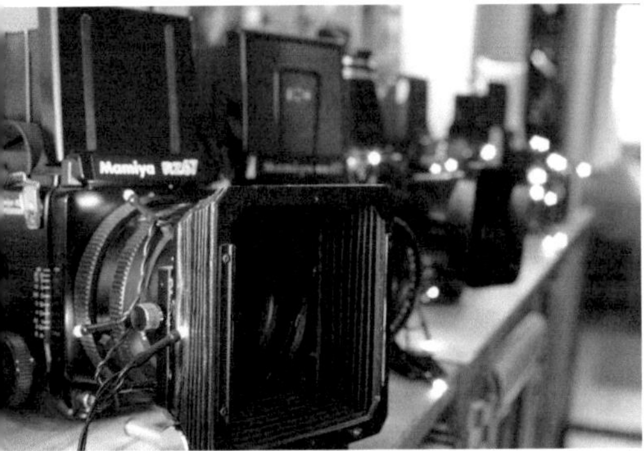

The topmost image, shot at f1.8, show only sharpness on the closest part of the bellows in the foreground. You can hardly see what camera it sits on. In the next image, shot at f8, you can recognize the camera. Finally, the last image, shot on f22, is almost sharp al the way to the background.

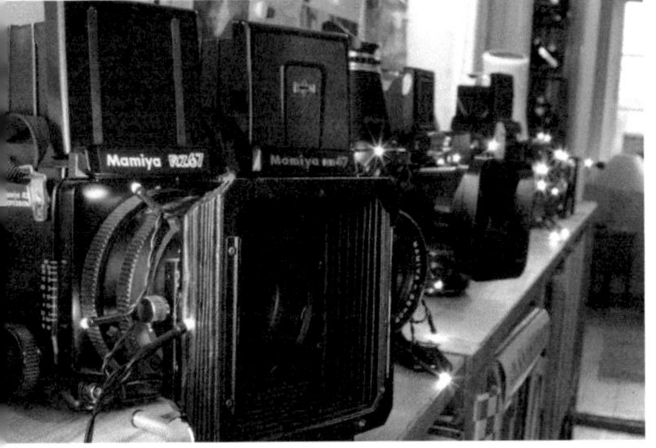

when shooting against the sun or street lights in the evening, or even create beautiful stars from reflected light in rain drops.

Actually, there are a few other things to note, in this case from the image shot at f1.8. One thing is that that the unsharp lights in the background are rendered circular near the image center, but they become elipsoidal as we move towards the image edge. The other thing to not, is that the unsharp lights here on the Canon 50mm lens are rendered quite evenly, but that is not always the case. Some lenses render such lights with an onion like structure with several concentric rings of light. Some will tend to like this effect, nevertheless, quality optics doesn't usually show this onion ring like structure, as it is considered a flaw.

In general I'm not afraid of optical defects or certain characteristics of lenses, as it can help create artistic images. Don't be sad if you lens renders onion rings in a setup like my example. On the contrary, learn to exploit it. I could point to many so-called optical defects that are actually great creative tools. I have already mentioned the Holga cameras and their completely imperfect lenses, and also the russian Helios lenses and their peculiar background blur, that photographers all over the World are excited about. But all these are optical flaws, that help create unique images.

There is one further thing, that I want you to note, shown in the middle image, even though it is also visible in the image shot at f22, just not so obviously. You can observe the shape of the aperture as the light is rendered as a shining pentagon. Also about this characteristic there is no agreement, some find it very distracting, others think it's cool. I'm sort of in the middle, as I find it can disturb an otherwise very pleasing landscape image, while in a creative image bubbling with colors and shapes it can add an extra artistic element.

Lenses and viewing angles

I have told you about lenses and their focal lengths, but haven't exactly described, what that means to you and the composition in your images.

Imagine a lens that gives a field of view like our own eyes, this lens is the so-called normal lens. The focal length of the normal lens is defined by the diagonal of the image format, which for 35mm film is 43.3 mm, but in daily use we denote anything between 40 and 55 mm a normal lens.

Now to telephoto and wideangle lenses. You know binoculars and their effect, both looking the "right" way through, but maybe also the puzzling effect, when looking the opposite way through. Used the normal way binoculars has an enlarging effect, and seems to draw distant objects closer, and that is the way telephoto lenses work. Looking the opposite way in the binoculars, the surroundings seem further away, which corresponds to the effect a wideangle provides.

Can we say anything about the effect of a certain focal length? If you have used a decent pair of binoculars with an enlargement of 8 times, that would correspond to a lens of 8 x 50 mm, ie 8 times the focal lenght of the normal lens and thus 400 mm. We would say this is a super tele. Most telephoto lenses for daily use have focal lengths in the interval from around 70 mm up to 200 mm ie an enlargement of 1½ to 4 times.

The opposite goes for the wideangle lens. On you camera objects seems further away, and thereby we have a size reduction. Using extreme wideangles like fish eye lenses, even rather near objects seem pretty far away.

The image series is taken with several wideangle settings via a normal lens setting to several telephoto settings.

How then does the focal length of the lens relate to image angle? The table on next page shows the relation between focal length and the horisontal image angle, and the same is illustrated graphically together with the definition lens groupings.

Often it is stated, that your lens changes the perspective, but that is actually not correct. What changes

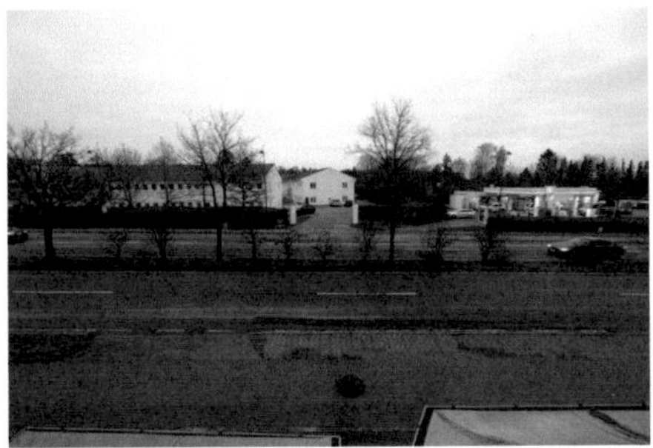

Wideangle lens (zoom) at 17mm

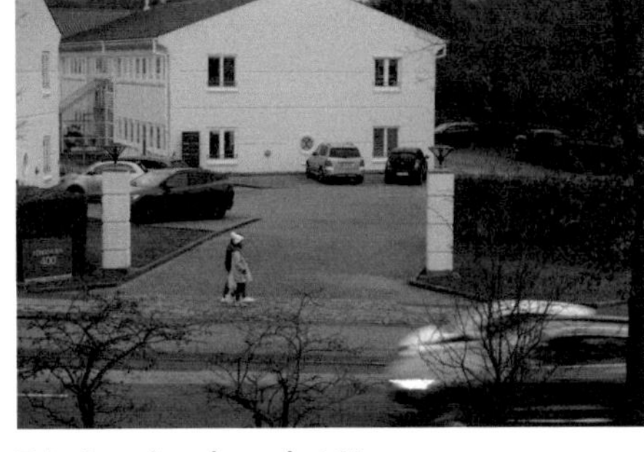

Telephoto lens (zoom) at 85mm

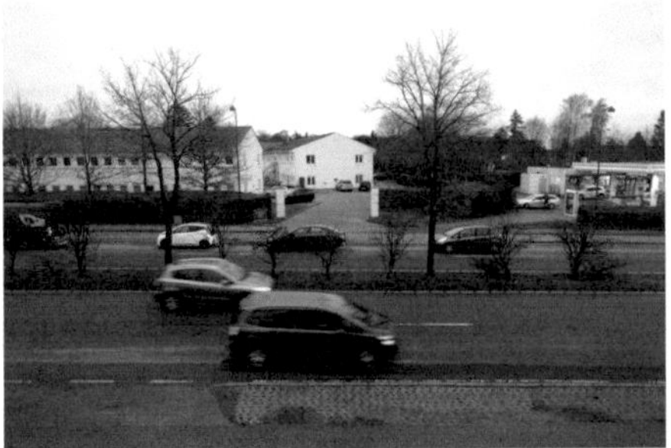

Wideangle lens (zoom) at 24mm

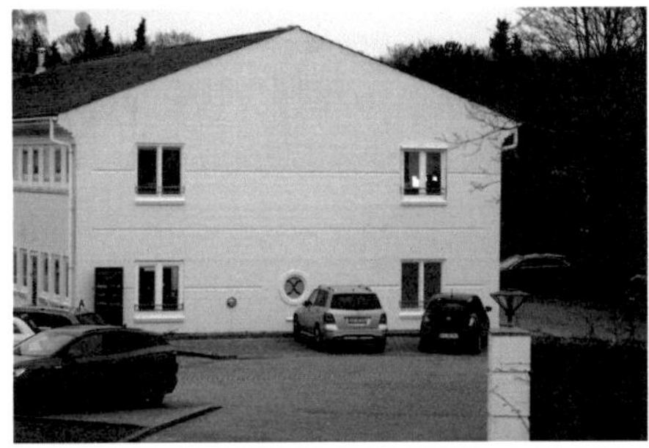

Telephoto lens ((zoom) at 135mm

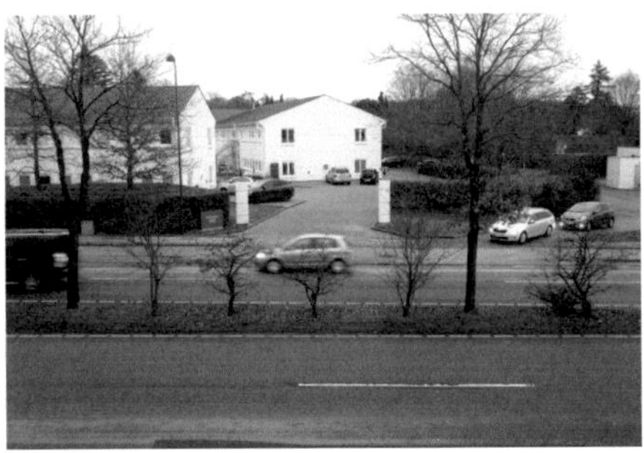

Wideangle lens (zoom) at 35mm

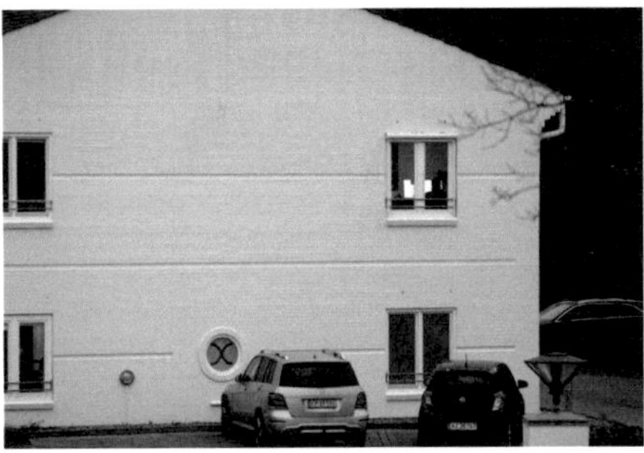

Telephoto lens ((zoom) at 200mm

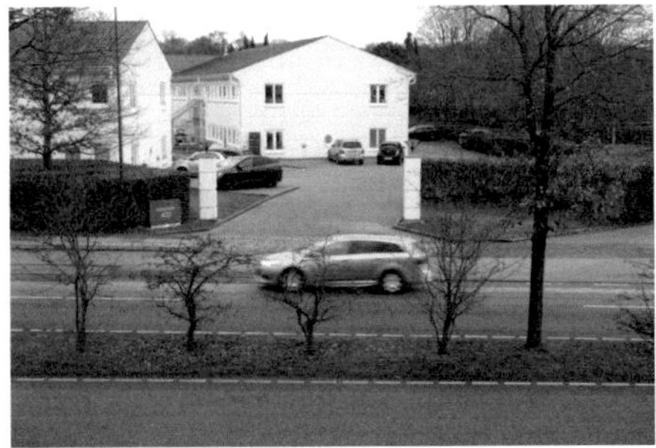

Normal lens at 50mm

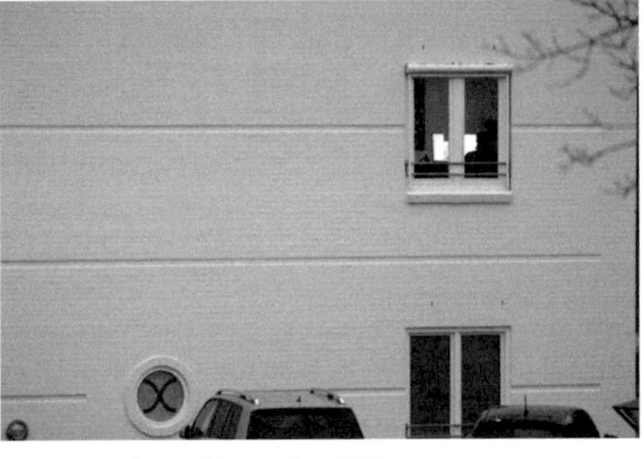

Telephoto lens ((zoom) at 300mm

the perspective is, if you move when changing your lens, in order to make your motive take up the same space in the image as before the lens change. Then the surroundings will change size in relation to your motive, thus changing the perspective.

Lets go with an example. You want to portray a person, but you like to include the environment around.

Therefore, you change from a normal lens to a wideangle lens, and move closer to the person for her to take up enough space in the image. At the same time more of the surroundings are included, though at the same time not occurring very prominent.

The image series show the change in perspective, and the relative sizes of motive versus surroundings, when you move in order for your motive to maintain its size - here the motive is a buddha statues in my guest room.

We'll discus this much more in the following sections on different shooting scenarios.

Focal length in millimeters	Horisontal angle
14	102.7°
16	95.1°
20	82.4°
24	73.7°
35	54.4°
50	39.6°
70	28.8°
85	23.9°
105	19.5°
200	10.3°
300	6.87°
400	5.15°
500	4.12°

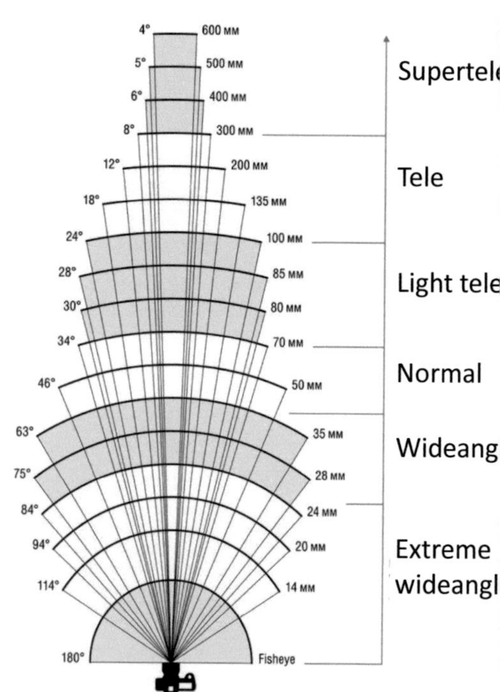

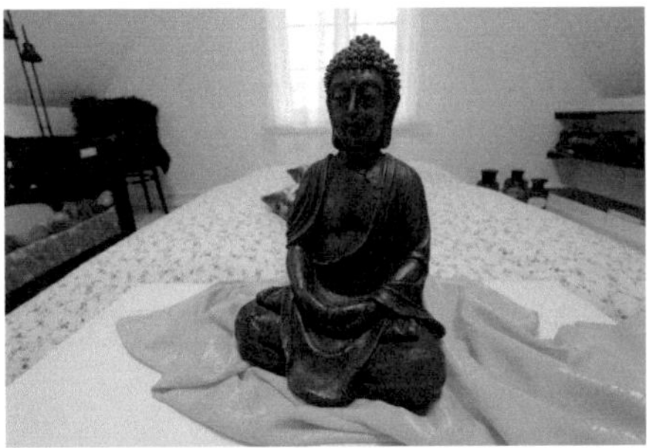
Wideangle lens (zoom) at 17mm

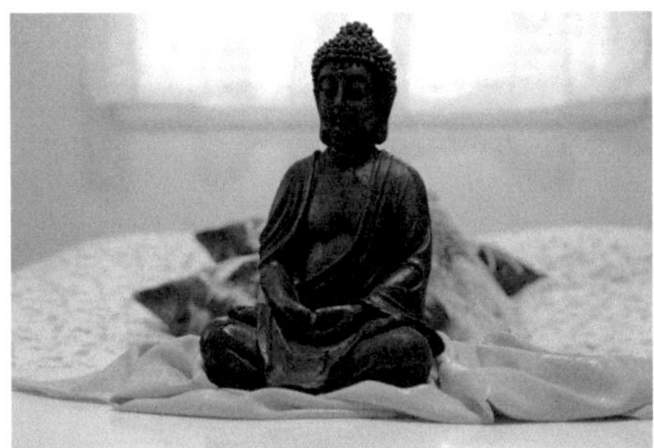
Telephoto lens ((zoom) at 85mm

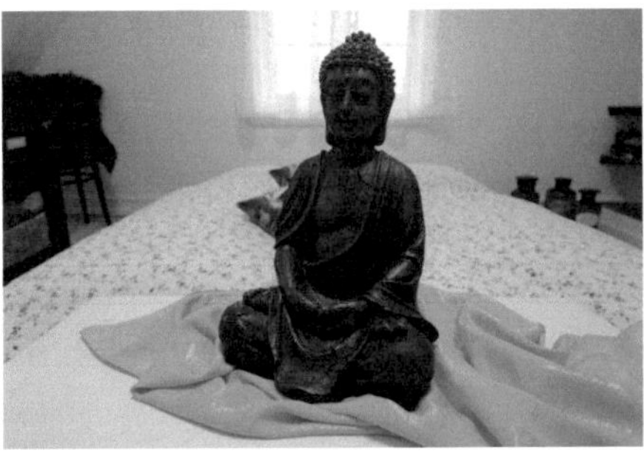
Wideangle lens (zoom) at 24mm

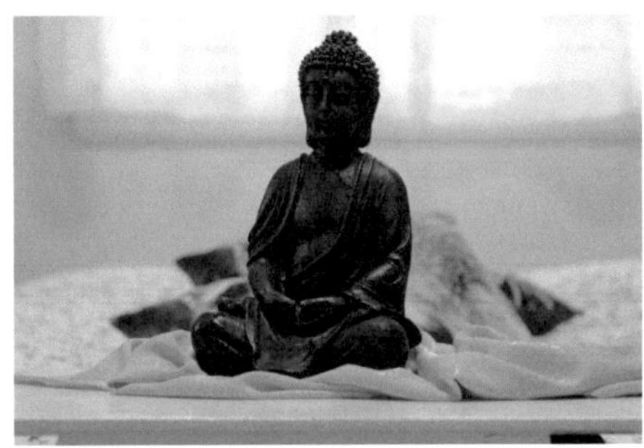
Telephoto lens ((zoom) at 135mm

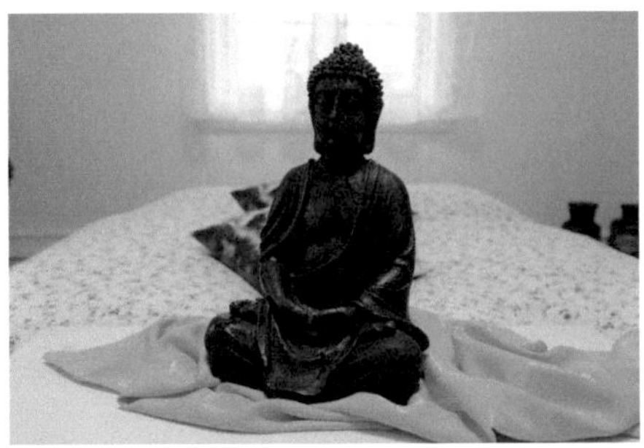
Wideangle lens (zoom) at 35mm

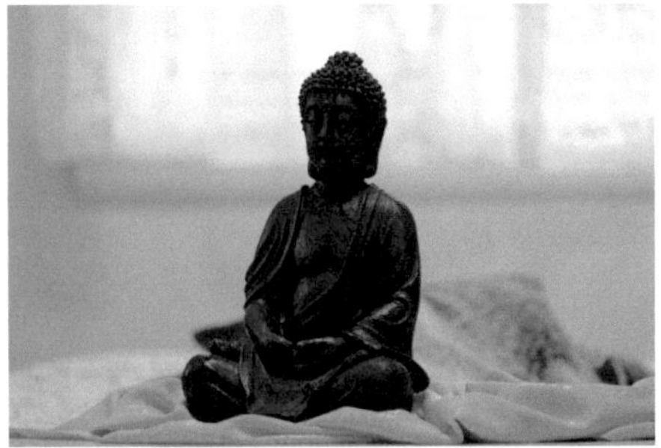
Telephoto lens ((zoom) at 200mm

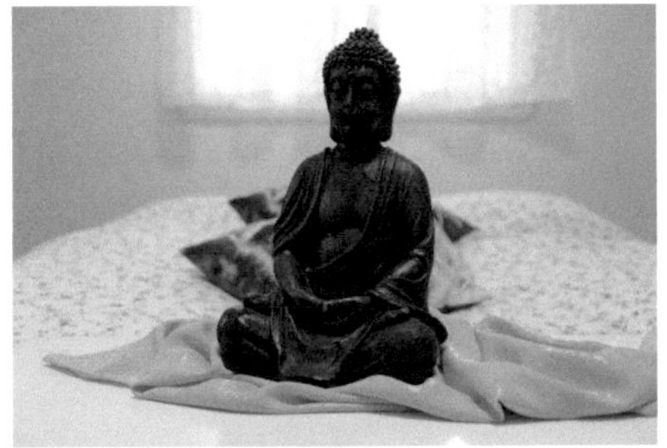
Normal lens at 50mm

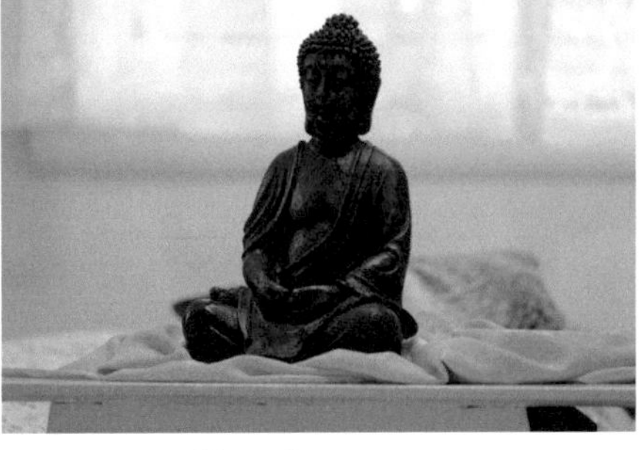
Telephoto lens ((zoom) at 300mm

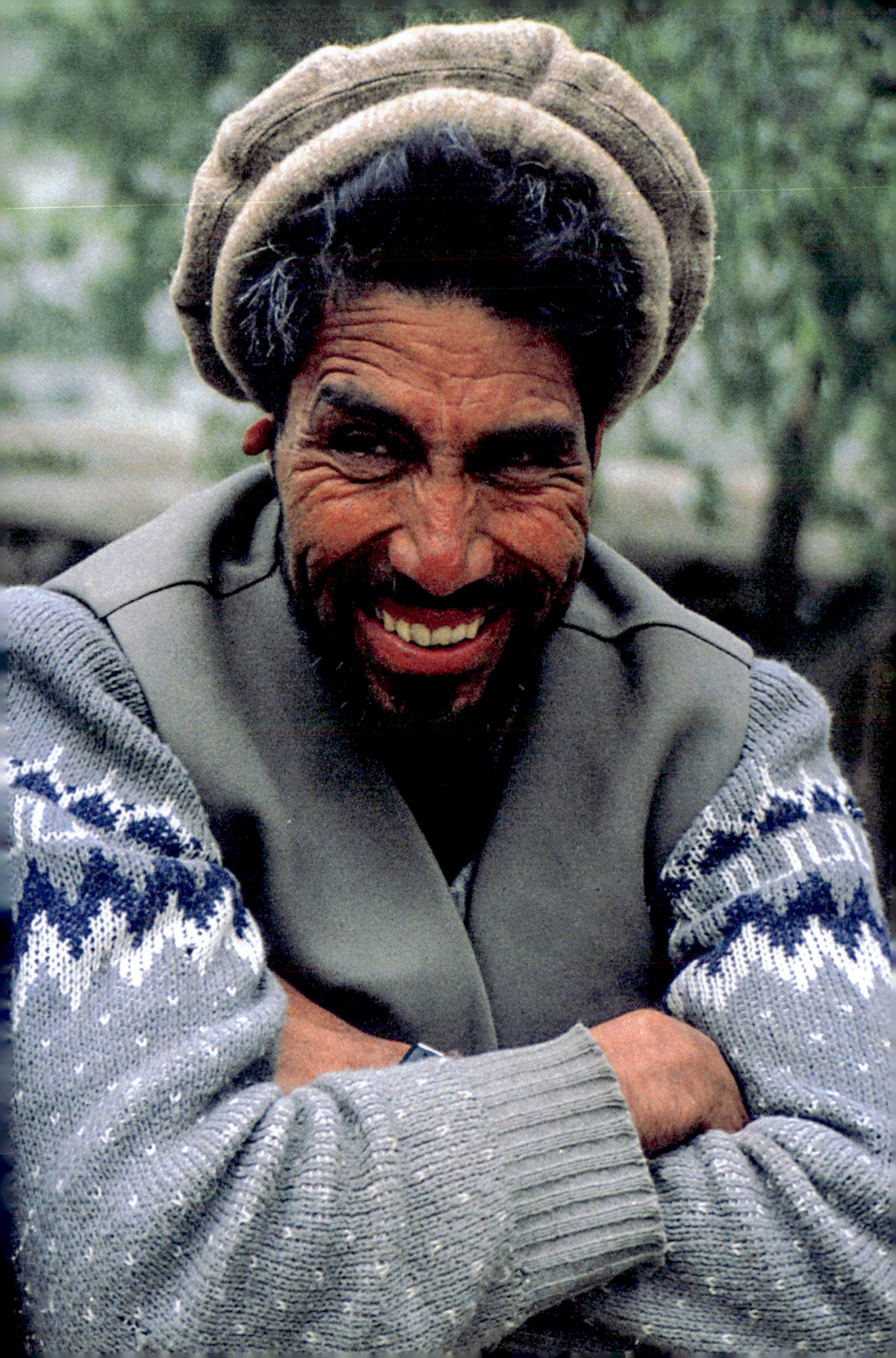

Portrait

We have already looked into depth of field, which is an important concept to understand, when shooting portraits. Here we'll introduce some further necessary considerations.

The opposite image is a portrait of one of our very strong and expressive porters on our way against the mountains in Northeastern Pakistan.

He is a man of the Balti tribe, that has their home in the problematic area bordering between Pakistan and India. He had an air of pride and calm in spite - or maybe exactly because of - the tough life these people live in the harsh mountain areas. Either you work hard in the field, going about agriculture the way we did in Europe 100 years ago, or you work for the visiting westeners. Nevertheless, that is also a very tough job.

The image is shot on my first semiprofessional SLR, a Nikon F90X using a Konica color positive film - ie. slide film. Actually, this type of film is not at all suited to the contrasty light in the mountains, as slide film has a very small latitude, resulting in either burned highlights or completely black shadows. On the other hand, going into the shadows under a tree, you can get less contrasty, well lit images with beautiful colors.

We on the expedition had to use slide film, as we knew we would do many lectures after the expedition - yes at that time there were no large screen projectors, we used slide projectors. Thus, we had to get the best from the film material we had for our trip to the summit of the 11. highest mountain in the World.

The lens was a socalled kit lens, albeit a decently sharp kit lens, covering a range from 35-70mm. Today that would be considered a very small coverage, but early zooms had lots of optical flaws, and couldn't cover more without being technically unusable. For portraits a 50mm lens with a wide aperture (f1.8 - f1.2) would have been a much better choice, but I couldn't carry that much equipment. Furthermore, I lacked a flash, none was build-in to this camera.

Good choices, when going for portraits, are either aperture priority or manuel exposure, as in these two modes you decide what aperture is used, and thus if the background should be rendered sharp, pretty unsharp, or totally blurred.

Good lightning is important for images, but decisive at portraiture, nevertheless, it can be created rather easily. If the shooting session takes place outdoors in bright sun, it can be a good idea to move into the shadow of a tree or something else. The direct light from the sun gives ugly, sharp shadows, not flattering for your model. Additionally, shooting in side light, or if your model has the light directly into her eyes, she will be squinting, not very beautiful. Furthermore, that usually gives wrinkles around mouth, eyes, and in her forehead. All in all not good for pleasing results.

A small detail is how to create life in the eyes of your model. It can be done with the help of a flashlight, fired on low power, not enough to lighten the model, just providing a small visible light in the eyes. If you still have deep shadows in the face of your model, you can turn up the power of the flashlight a bit to soften up the shadows.

The placement of focus is equally important, as a portrait where the eyes aren't sharp will seem odd. If your camera has autofocus, you should place the active focus area over one of the models eyes, before pressing the shutter button - or the focus lock button, if you have such one. If the portrait is shot right on, it is not important if its one eye or the other, but a general rule is, if one of the eyes are closer, you should focus on that eye.

By many portraiture is perceived as limited to the head and a minor part of the upper body, but definitely with focus on the face. Factually, there are lots of portraits just like described, but a portrait can include the whole body. If you think about one of the most famous portraits in the World, the portrait of Mona Lisa in Louvre, Paris, that shows most of the upper body and how she rests her hands in her lap. Obviously, that is much more than the traditional limited perception of a portrait.

On this page and the opposite I try to show the difference between a portrait and the environmental portrait.

The image below of a peasant in the mountains of Ladakh is a typical portrait, shot relatively close up, and not showing much of the surroundings, although it seems to be shot indoors, but we can't be too sure. For certain is that the peasent is hardened by a life in the mountains, obviously he has used himself during the years.

Opposite we meet the peasant outside his house, and we gain a bit of insight into how he lives. We also see his stature, see that his back seems bend by years of work in the field, but it is only by inference, as nothing shows this. Portraing this man could have been completed by showing him behind the plough pulled by oxen, then we would know much more about him.

This way these two kind of portraits complements each other to convey the full story of the portrayed.

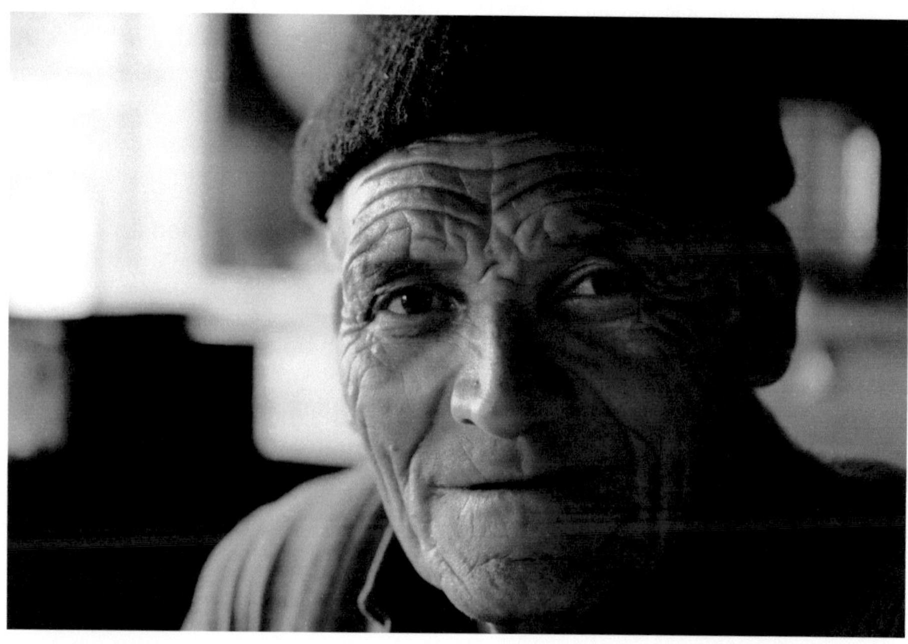

Environmental portrait

If we take the definition of an "environmental portrait," then many of the portraits we usually make will belong in this category. Whereas a "portrait" is a depiction of the physical appearance of a person, then the current category is as much a depiction of the environment that surrounds the person, that be the private sphere or the occupational sphere.

Contrary to a portrait, where we often try to hide or blur the surroundings, in the environmental portrait we include recognizable elements of the environment, where the subject is at home.

In the private sphere it could be your husband in the kitchen, clearly preparing the dinner, and showing the kitchen and the tools that are carefully chosen to be part of the story, the image tells.

In the work sphere it could be the somewhat unusual female carpenter, standing on the scaffolding with her tools, the image obviously showing this as part of the environmental portrait.

By including the environment in a way, that elements are fully recognizable, we take quite a different approach compared to the strict portrait, where we as creators use

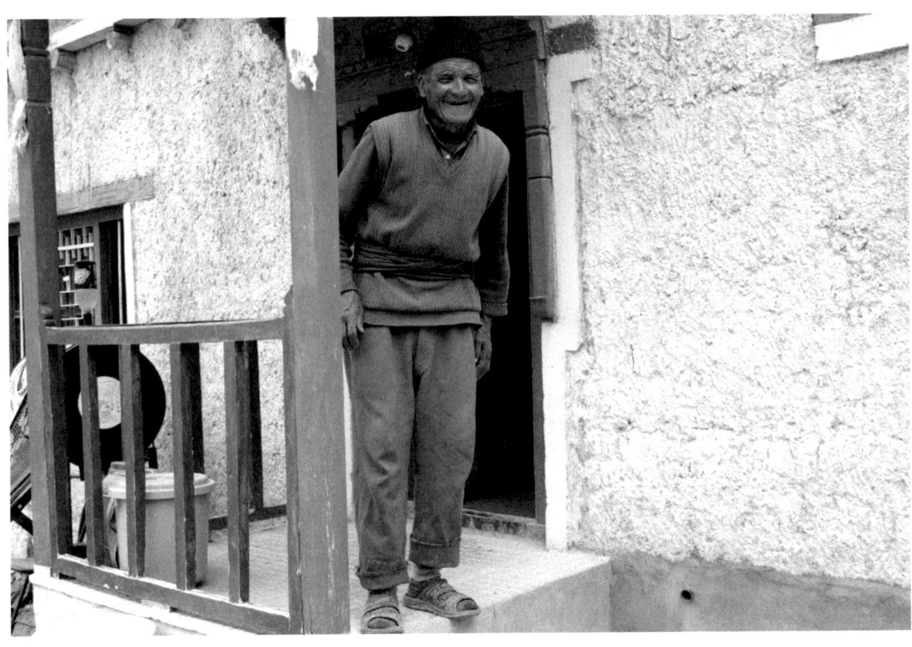

settings hiding the surroundings. Thus, for the environmental portrait, we will use camera and lens settings very much different from the ones used for the isolated portrait. We won't use the lowest aperture values in order to blur the background, and we won't use lenses, that only show the central part of the image sharply. Furthermore, we won't crop the image to only contain the subject, we will let the environment around take some space.

Both types of portraits can tell a lot. A portrait shot close up could for instance show the wrinkles of an older person, telling a story of a life full of hard work. The environmental portrait, shot a larger distance, might show a battered fishing boat, that the portraid was standing on, telling about the hard work.

Conclusively, the traditional portrait and the environmental portrait has each their own way of telling a story, and they can supplement each other. In the example above, the wrinkles in the face would strongly express the hard life of the person, and we could imagine many ways they could be acquired. As a photographer you could end the story there, but you might want to express more clearly, what kind of life the person had lived, and the environmental portrait can help to tell that part of the story.

While a short telephoto lens with a wide aperture, and its ability to isolate the subject, would be suitable for the portrait, a wide angle lens would more suitable for the environmental portrait.

A French mountaineer in front of a glacier in the Mont Blanc area. To a large extent, the image show the environment around, although focus in on her. Olympus Trip 35 on Fomapan 100 film.

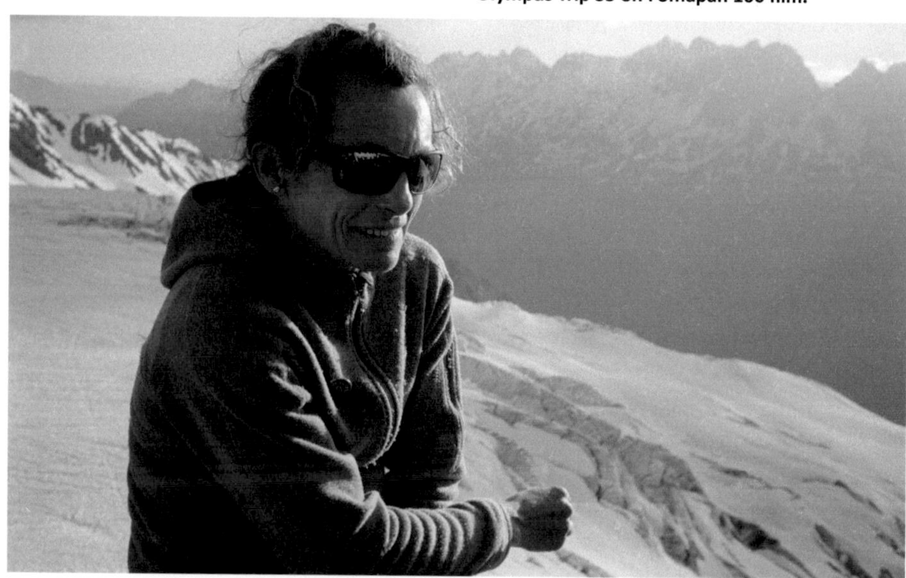

Landscape

Frankly, this category is very comprehensive. Thus, the photographic techniques has to be adapted to the landscape, and more importantly the way you want to depict it. Showing a landscape is not just about showing everything, but focusing on a certain part in a way chosen by you.

Therefore, the choice of technique (aperture, focal length, film sensitivity etc.), time of day, and thereby the light, as well as your viewpoint, are crucial for the final result.

Shooting landscapes it becomes obvious how important the right lighting is for your image. I have shot many pictures on my way through beautiful mountain landscapes in the middle of the day. There are none of these that belong to my favorite image, no matter how amazing the surroundings

The relation between humans and the landscape tells us a lot about the relative sizes, as seen in the image on this page and on the following pages.

The image on this page is shot using a slightly wide angled lens, same Olympus Trip 35 camera and Fomapan 100 film as the image on previous page. The lens is a 40mm. Although it is close to a normal lens, it creates focus on the persons in the foreground.

That is sharply opposed by the image on next page, created with a 100mm lens. The lens and the increased distance to the persons in the image gives more power to the imposing mountain wall in the background. Here the humans only work to increase the impression of the grandeur of the mountains. This can be increased even further by using even stronger telephoto lenses.

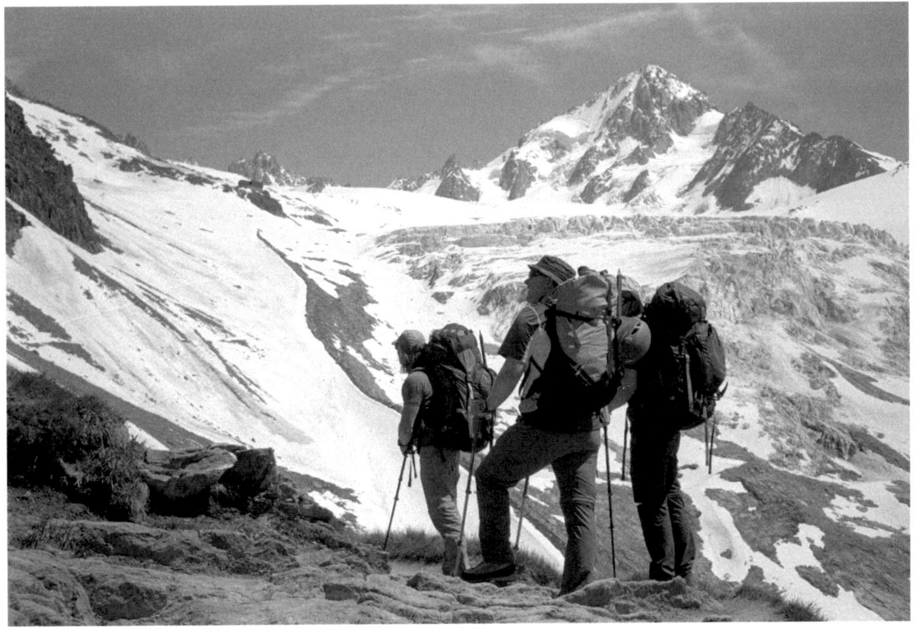

were. It is truly decisive to wait until the light hits in a way, that creates more depth in the scenery. Furthermore, in the beginning or the end of the day the light gives more warmth to the image. That is not to say that images must always look like sunsets, that's definitely not the point. The important point is to always be aware of the possibilities, and maybe prepared to visit the same place several times to catch the motive in the optimal light.

Sometimes eg on travels it is not possible, and then you must make the best of the conditions on the time of your visit. It might be, that a change of your viewpoint can exploit the lightning in a better way, or a change of technique can create a more pleasing and expressive image.

Again, the image on the opposite page aims to show how the human element can be used to increase the impression of the grandeur of nature. It depicts one of my former climbing partners in the middle of the gigantic and feared Everest icefall.

The image is shot on a simple point&shoot camera, a Konica Big Mini, on a slide film, subsequently converted to black and white. By this you also learn, that great images are not created by the camera but by the photographer and the situation you decide to document.

The spreads on the following double pages are of a completely different character. There is more "Zen" to the calm way nature has been shown, not disturbed by human elements. Both are shot on a Canon A-1 with a 35mm lens, respectively on Fomapan 100 b&w and Kodak Ektar 100 color film.

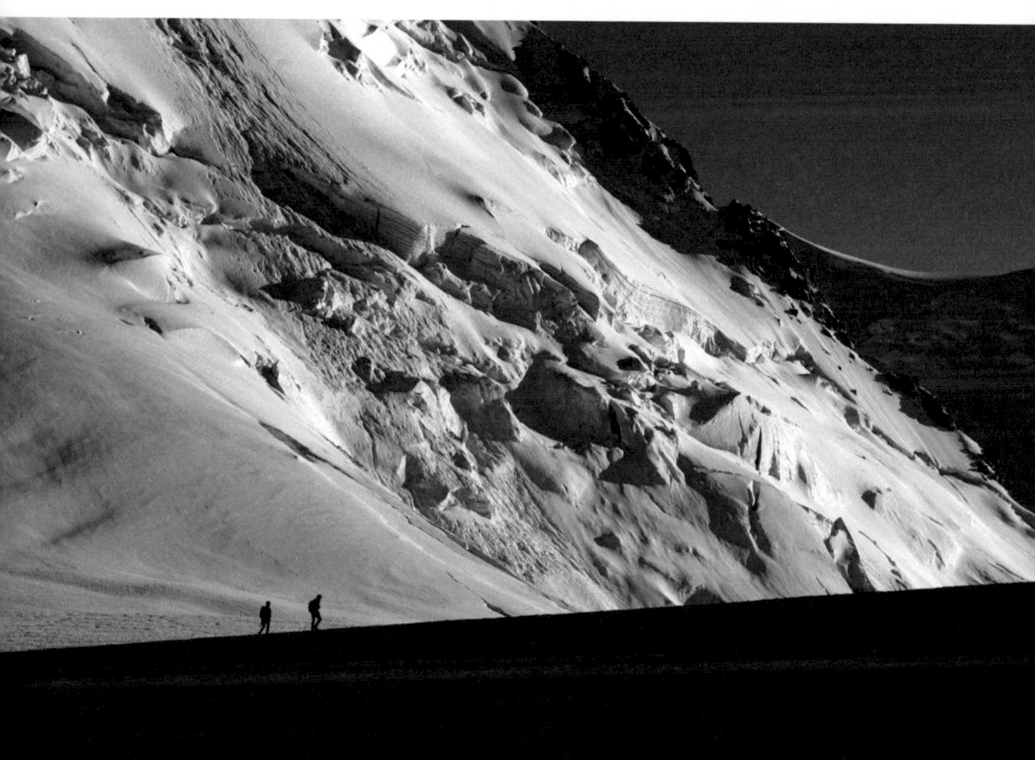

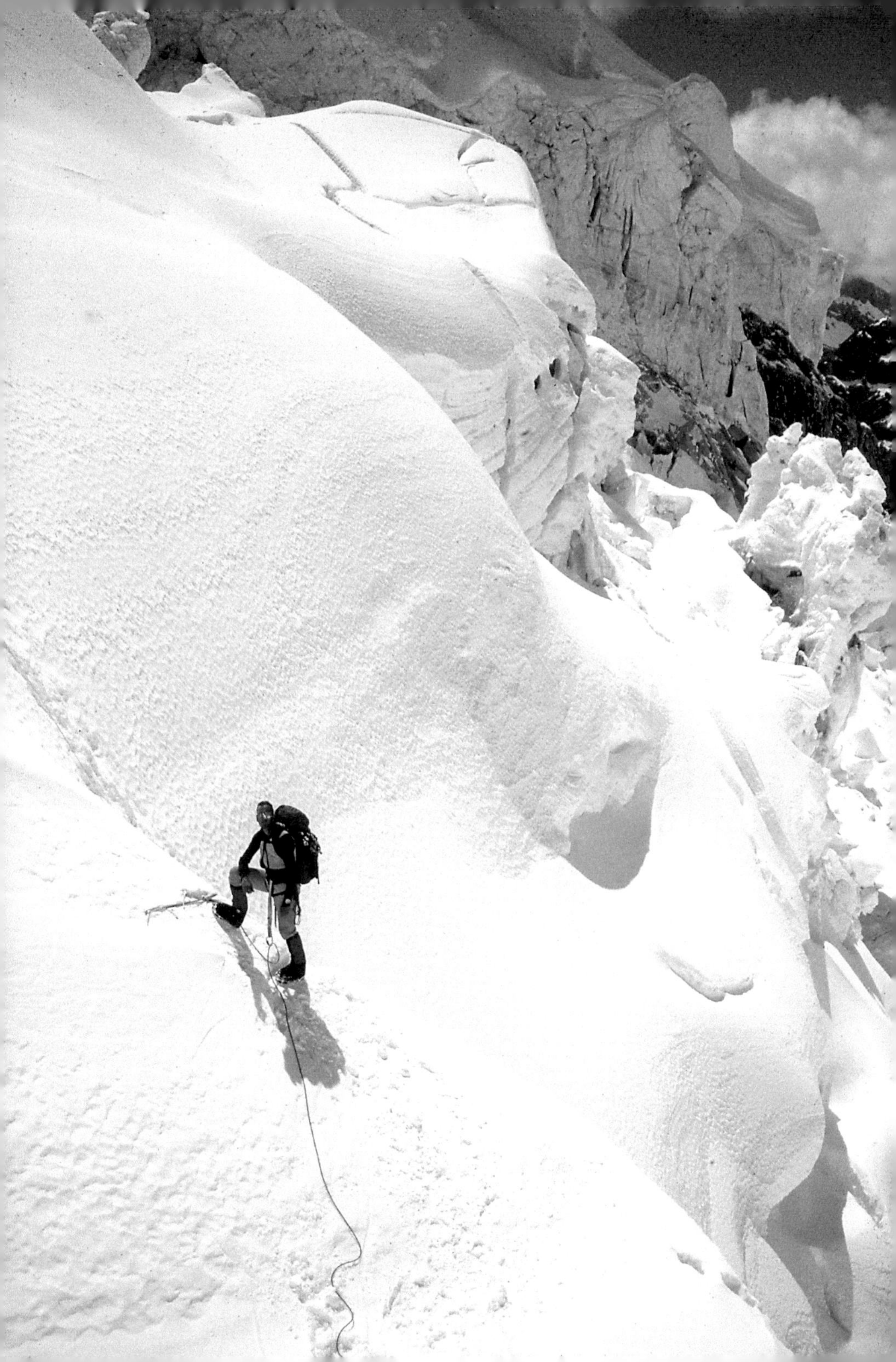

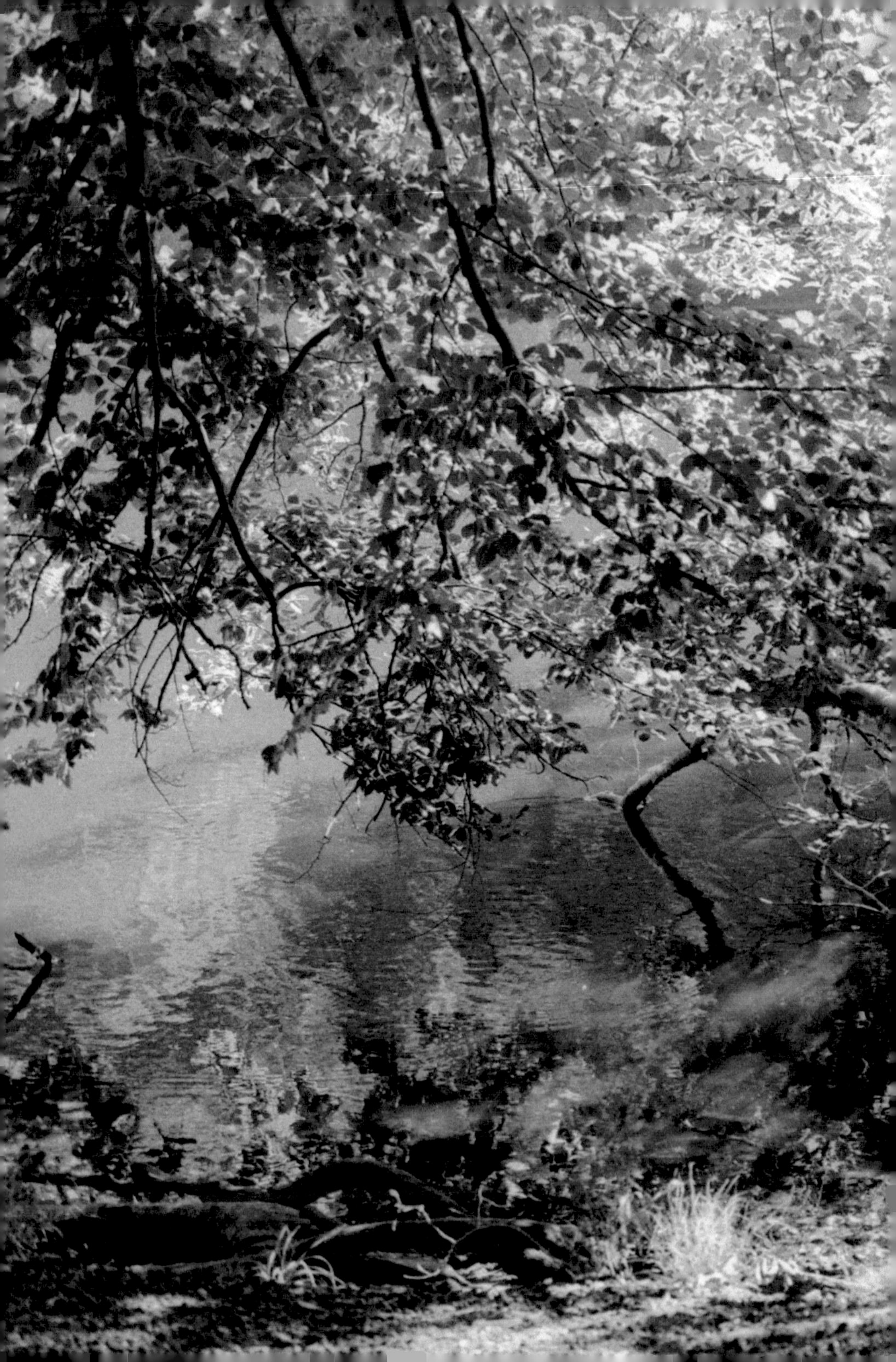

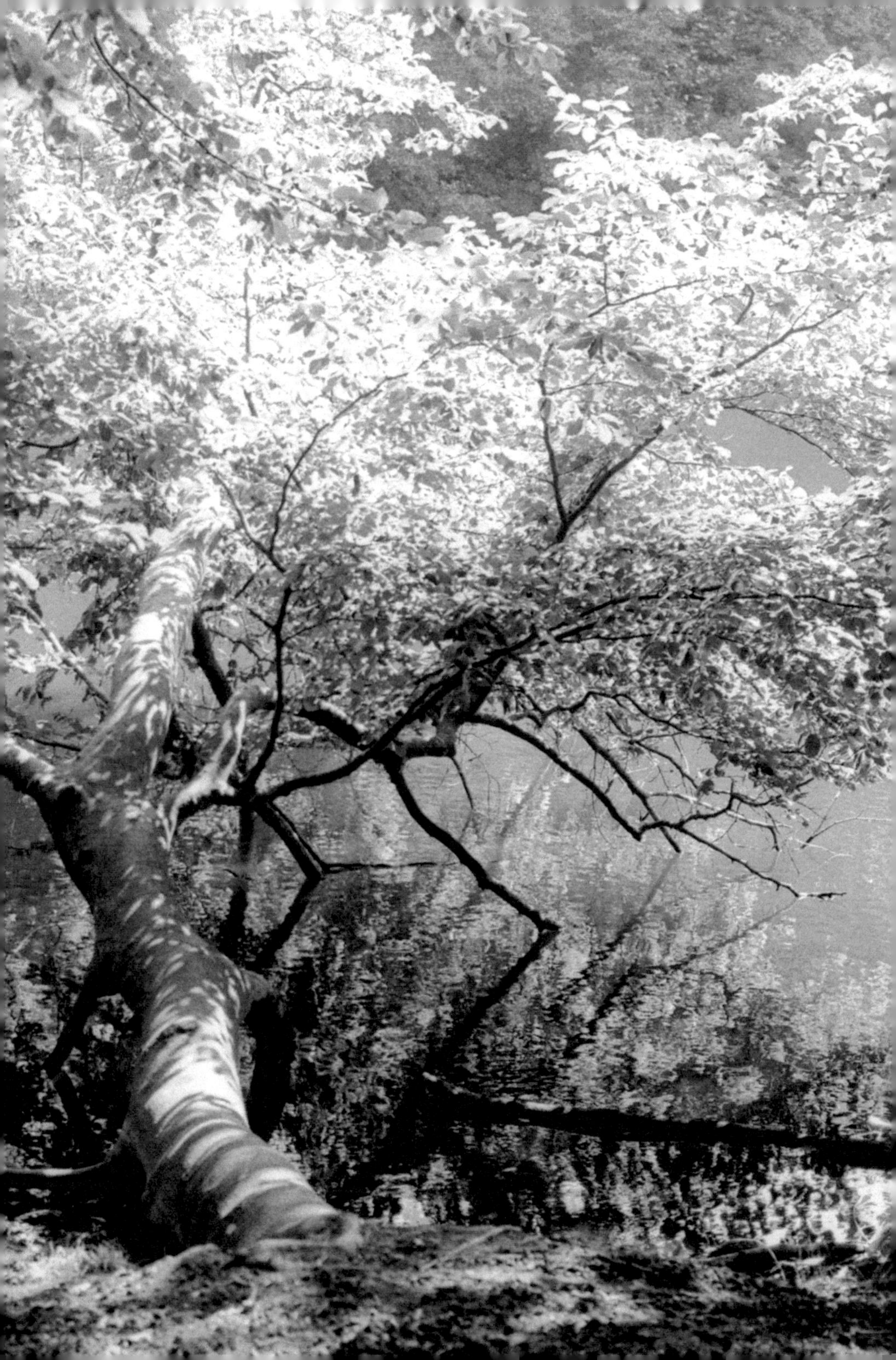

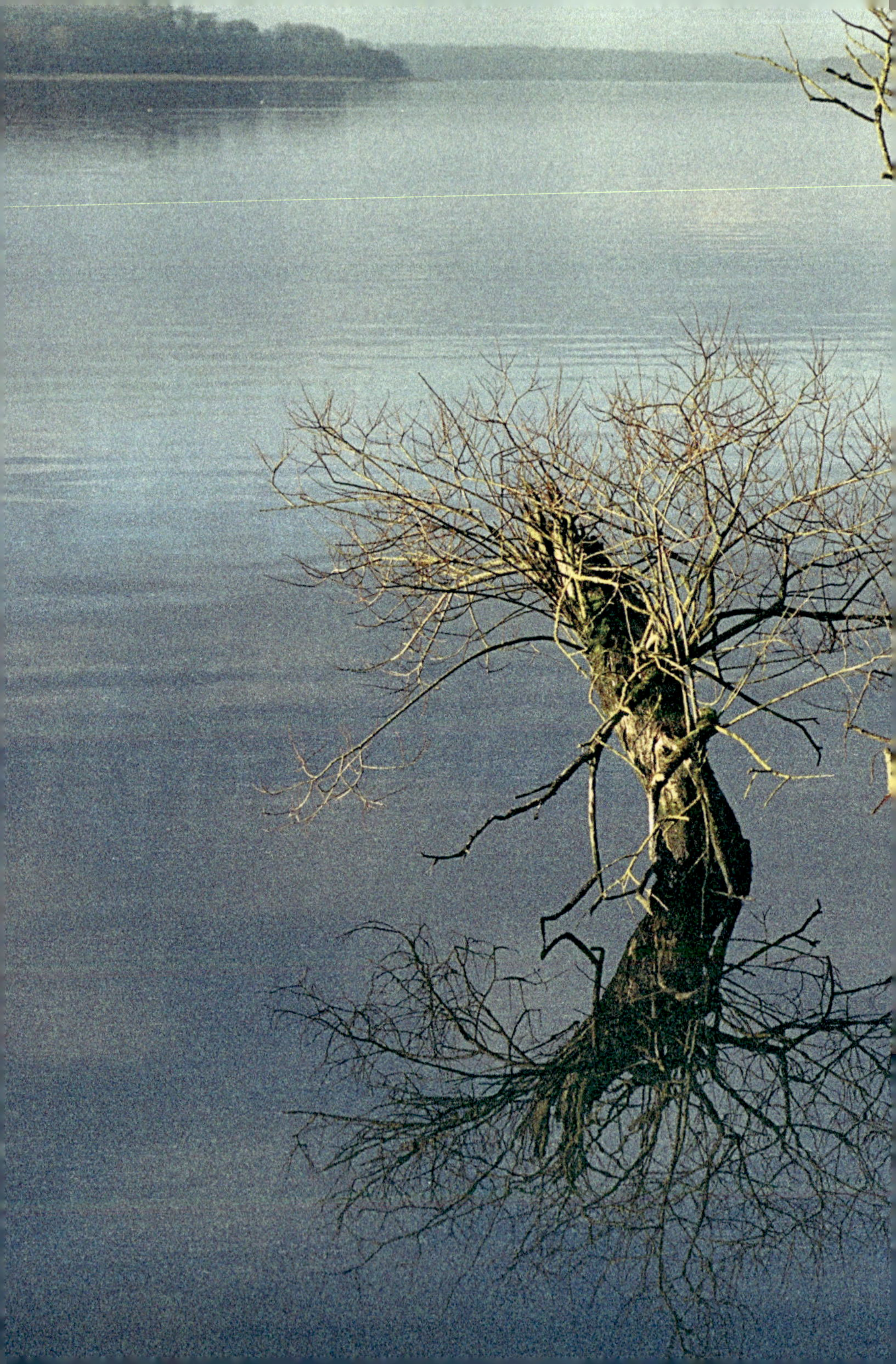

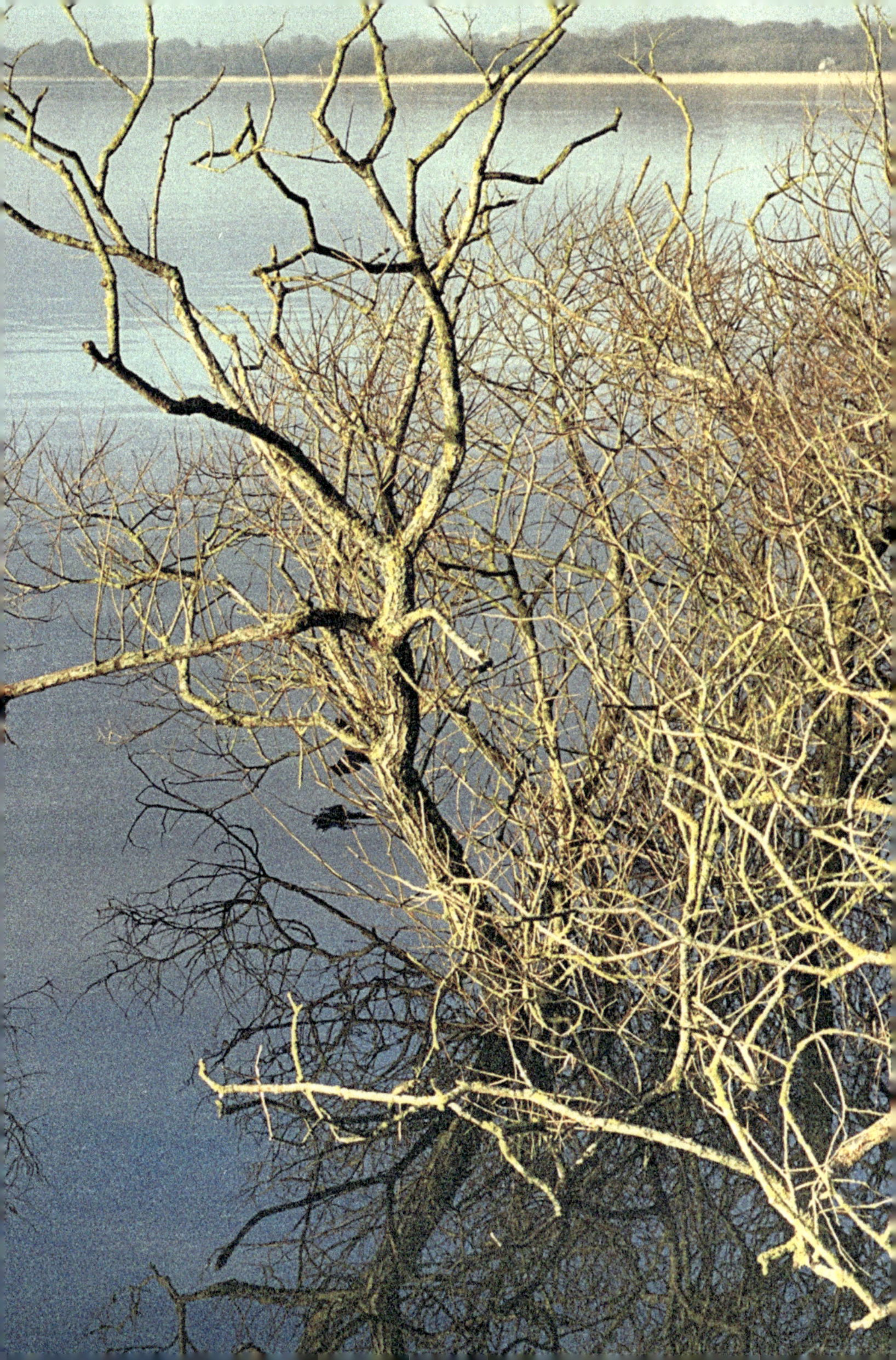

Street photography

The so-called "street photography" genre is also a wide field. For some it means that people explicitly has to be present in the cityscape, while others don't have this focus, but tend more to document the environment.

I'm not fond of strict definitions, my opinion being that you decide how you will perceive it. It is not important until you might some day decide to send your images to a photo competition, or just let others on Instagram judge your images. Then suddenly, their opinions become obvious, but don't let it frighten you, so far you decide yourself.

One thing that almost anyone can agree on is, that the camera for street photography should be as unobtrusive as possible, or be so retro it automatically gets acceptance by people in the street.

Partly for that reason on of my favorite cameras, that you have already seen images from earlier, the Olympus Trip 35, is one of the best. Reason being that it is a small, retro camera, but at the same time a camera that is easy to use and usually provides pleasing images.

That is exactly what you want, when you wander the city, and has focus on spotting exciting motives, and get them in the box before they are gone.

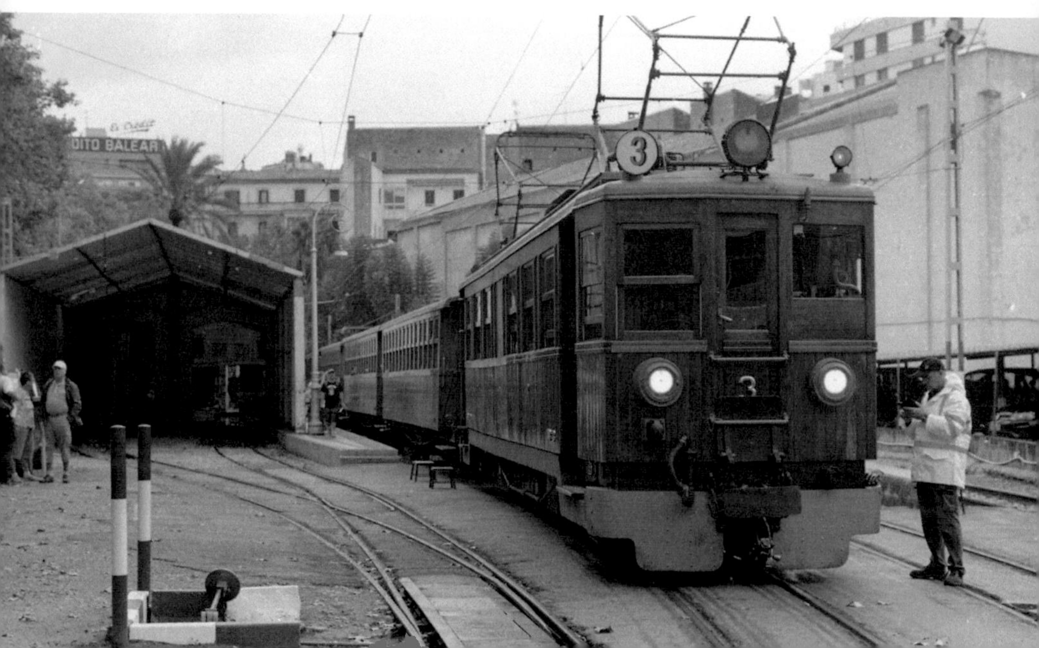

The railway station in La Palma, where the train starts towards Soler on the north side of Mallorca. The old train is exciting and a tourist attraction due to its age and the terrain it runs through.

Nevertheless, other types of cameras are also usable. I have shot street photography using middle format cameras, that are pretty large. However, I have used the so-called waist level finder, which means I don't have to hold the camera in front of my face, hiding myself behind it. I believe that leads to the acceptance of being photographed.

Now we are at it, you must remember, that if your images will be published in any kind, your are actually obliged to get acceptance from the person(s) in your image, if they are recognizable. You can freely photograph in public places without getting permission from people in your scene, if they are anonymous in the final image. If that is something, that worries you, I think you should explore the rules a bit more, than just reading my brief advice here.

A bit more on equipment. Photographing at dusk makes it important to consider the light gathering capability of you lens. The mentioned type of camera might not be sufficient, as the lenses usually not has very wide apertures. Somewhat more expensive models like the Canon Canonet QL17 with its f1.7 aperture could come in handy.

Alternatively, a SLR with a wide aperture lens could be necessary. You can get lenses with apertures down to f1.4 without it needs to cost a fortune. Lenses even down to f1.2 and below exists, but they are often so excessively expensive, that they are out of reach.

Passengers on their way into the train on the opposite page. Both images are shot on a Canon AE-1 program using a 50mm f1.4 lens, a lovely compact setup, that I adore. Unfortunately, the price of both has skyrocketed lately. The images are shot on one of my favorite film, the Fomapan 100, that is both relatively fine grained, easy to develop, and furthermore it is cheap.

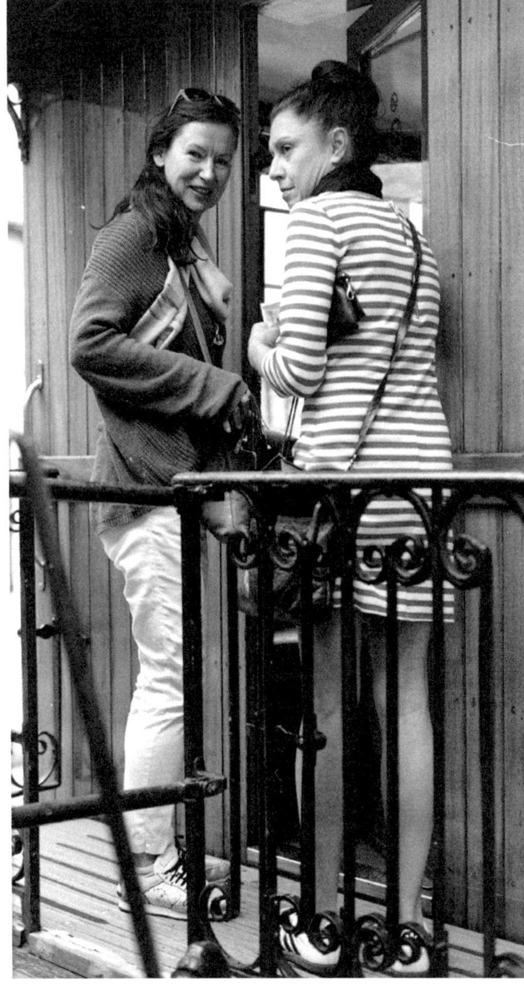

Action photography

Compared to other genres in photography there are not so many rules as to what is actually action photography. At least it must concern some kind of activity, often also moving objects but not strictly so.

Are you documenting motor sports, no one will argue that you are an action photographer. Most people regard my images from the mountains as action, though I tend to regard them more as nature photographs, or, when I move close to people, as environmental portraits. On the other hand when I'm shooting climbing, that is definitely action photography.

Obviously, as can be concluded from the above there is a transition zone. When is it "only" mountaineering and more like nature photography, and when is it climbing and action?

These two images from my career as combined photographer, mountaineer, and climber must clearly be defined as action photography.

Below my climbing partner through many years, Jan Mathorne, with whom I reached many of my most challenging goals, is climbing on the Frendo pillar in the Mont Blanc range. A day that ended in heavy fog before reaching the summit.

Opposite, two to us unknown climbers ascend a route parallel to ours on Mont Blanc du Tacul. I had an unobstructed view towards them, and used any possible moment to photograph them.

Both images are shot using a Konica point&shoot camera, and are shot on Konica slide film.

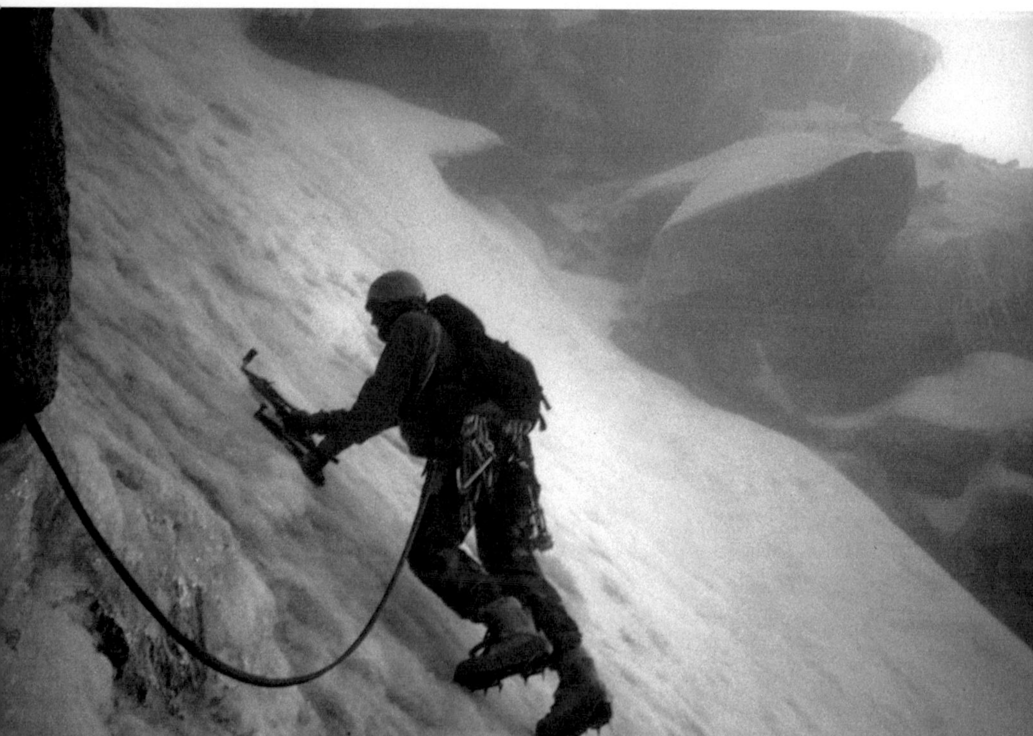

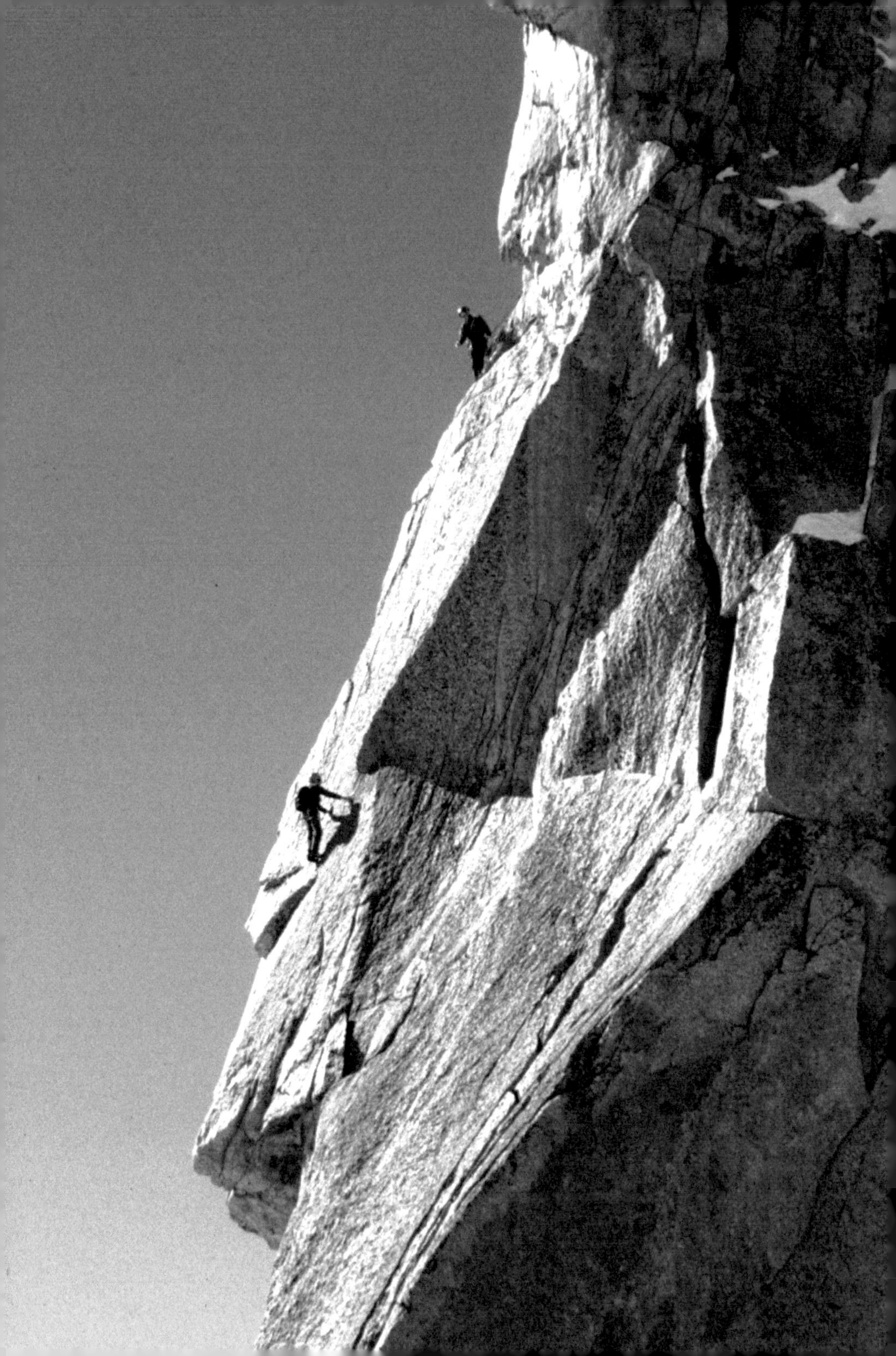

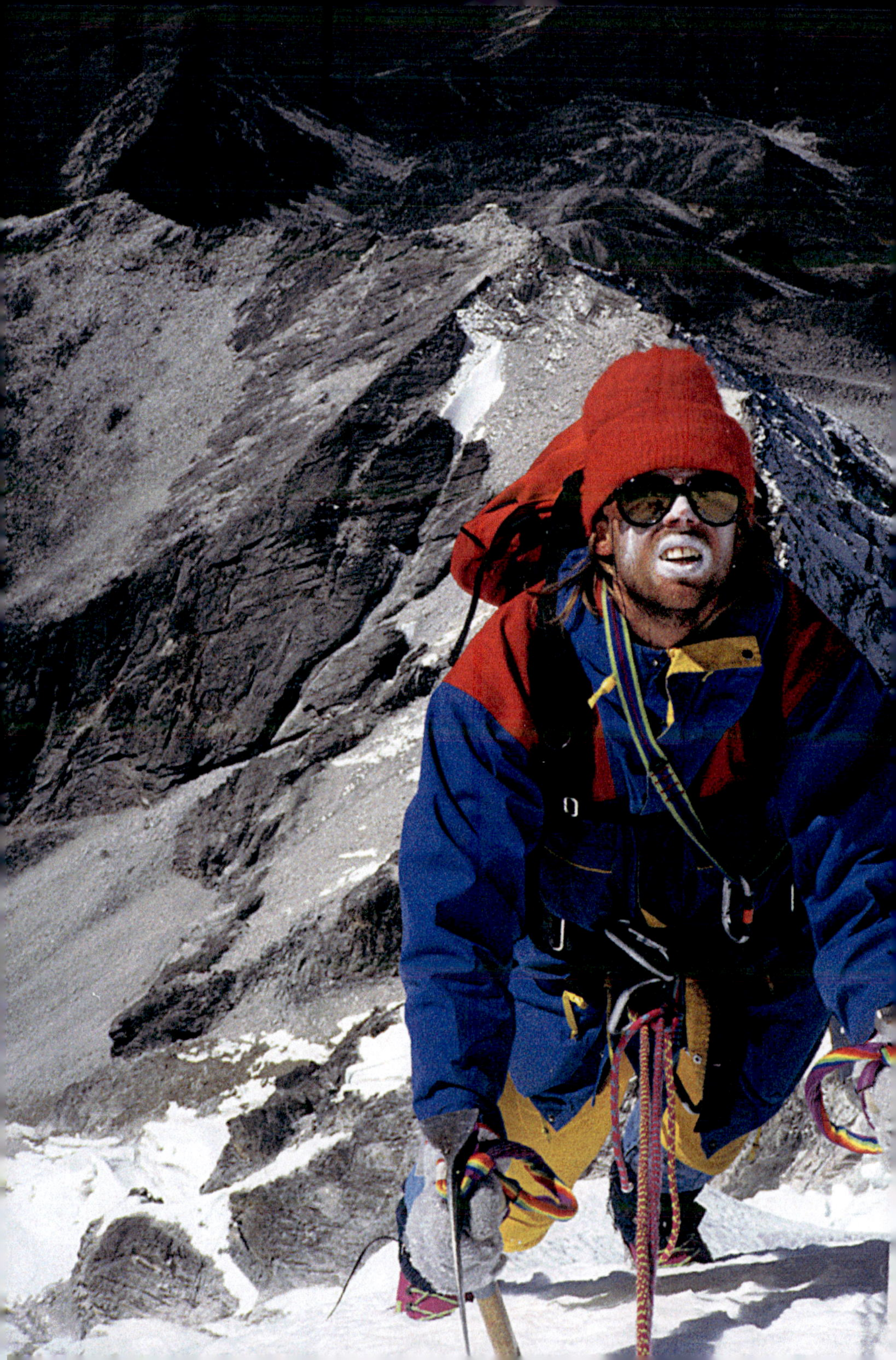

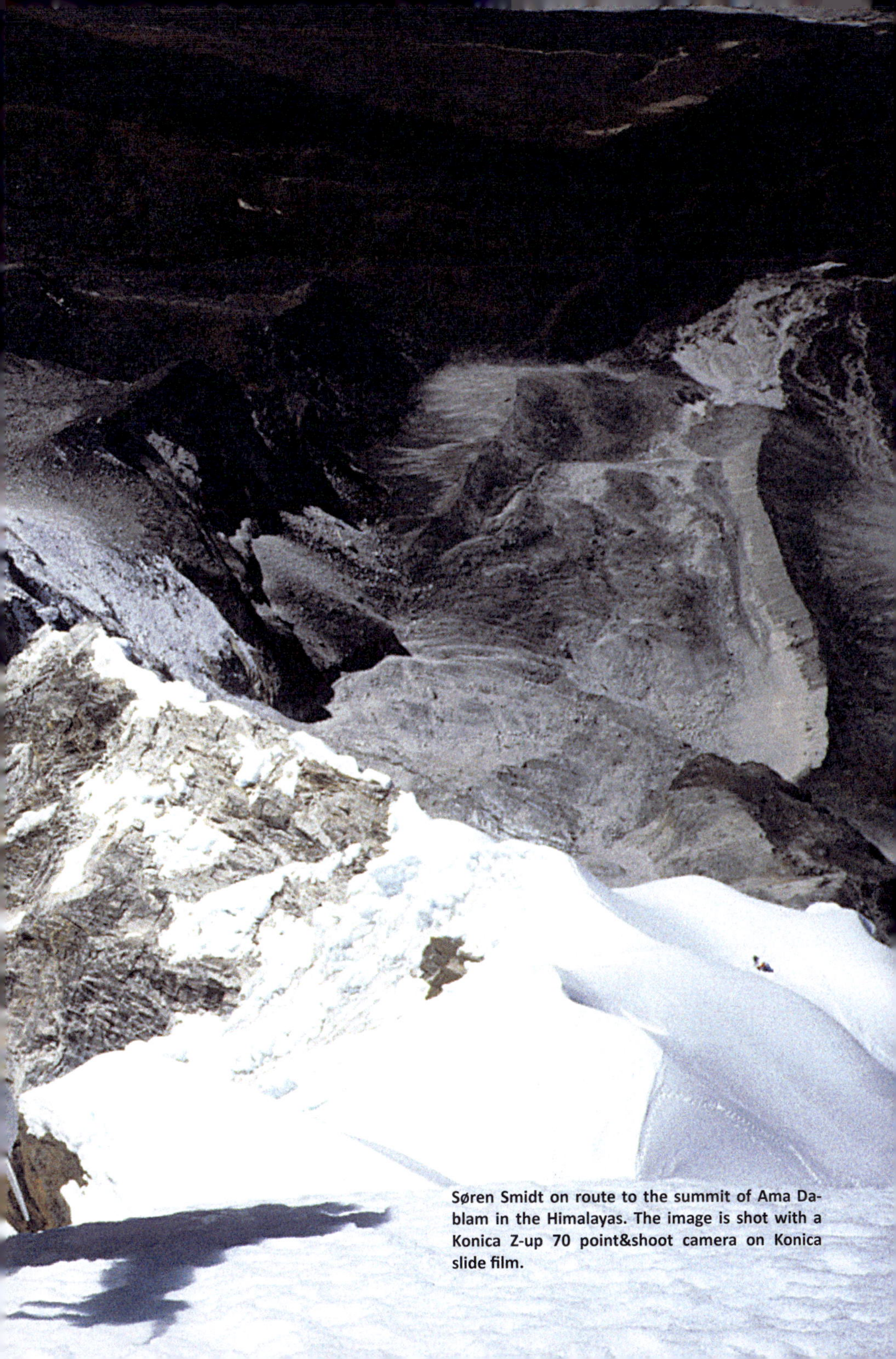

Søren Smidt on route to the summit of Ama Dablam in the Himalayas. The image is shot with a Konica Z-up 70 point&shoot camera on Konica slide film.

The above is only for your information, now you know when shooting action, that other photographers would sometimes say, that your images are not action photography. Nevertheless, as was the case with street photography, that only matters for instance if you enter a competition with your images, as you will have to fit within the theme for the competition, or to the category that you are participating in.

The equipment for action photography can vary quite a lot, but I'll go with some examples. The image of the kayakers is shot with a Konica Mermaid camera, a waterproof camera, that I'we also used in the mountains in order to shoot in extreme weather conditions. In principle it is a point&shoot camera without many settings to change.

The image of my son in law and my daughter on a slackline is shot with an SLR using a 50mm lens. The shutter time was 1/125 second, but it doesn't need to be that fast, as you would like to see a bit of movement, like in his arms. The movement in the image, and the diagonal composition adds to the dynamics of this image.

The last image is filled with motion, shot at 1/20 sec. I panned following the girl to blur the background. The lens was a 40mm.

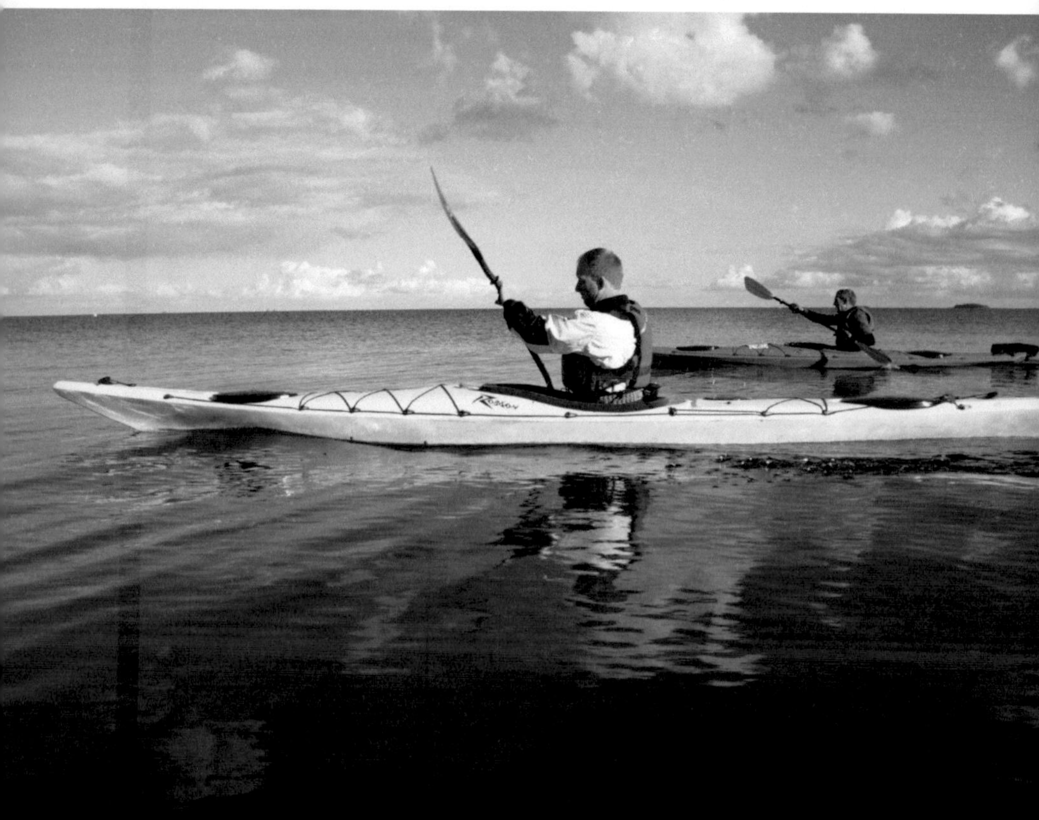

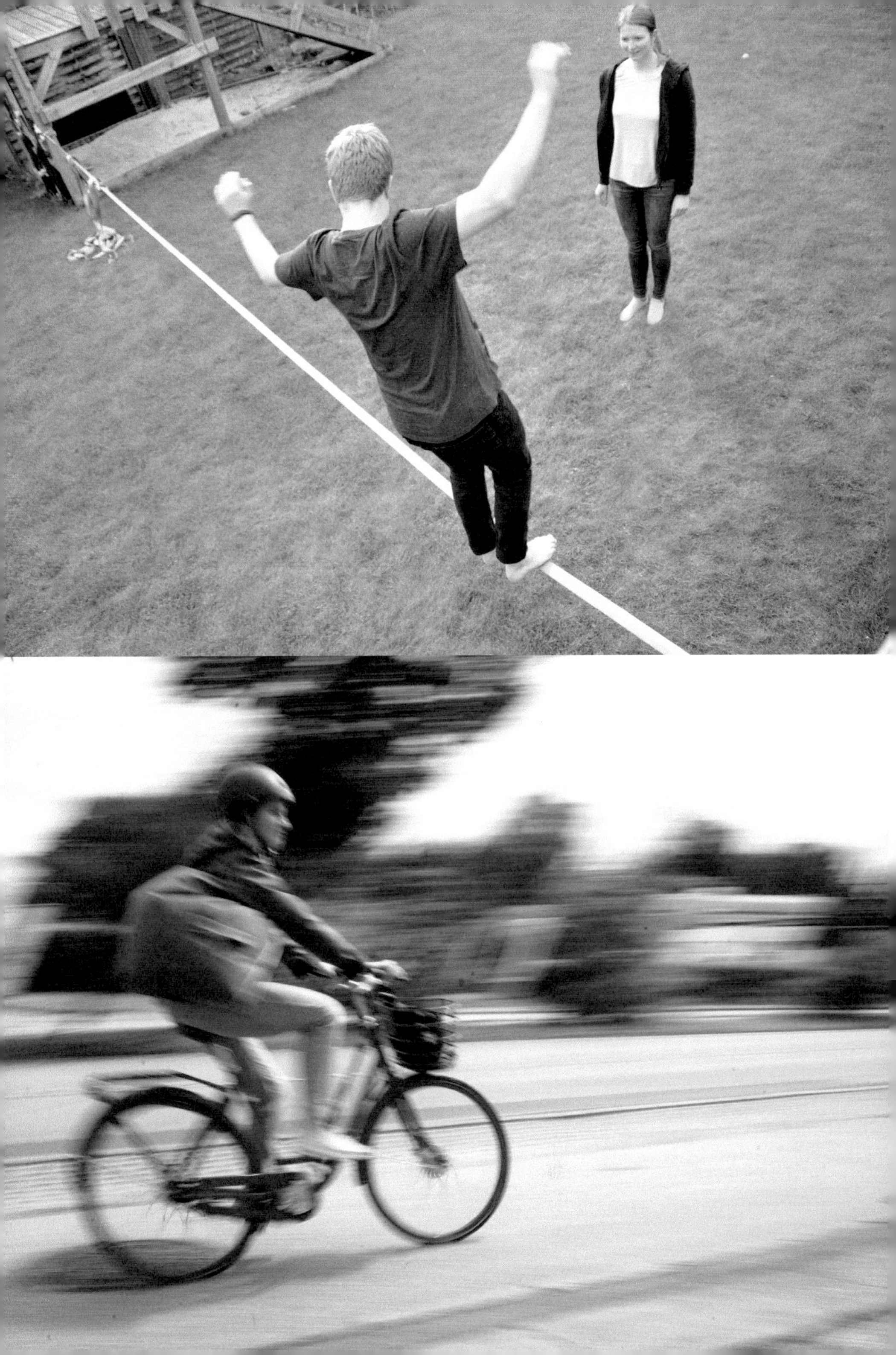

Macro photography

Lets start with the strict definition of macro, which states that if your setup are capable of reproducing 1:1 or larger, ie that the objects on the film (or sensor in digital photography) are as large as in reality or larger, we are in macro territory. But again I find the definition to limiting, and to me macro is just photographing small objects and details of larger objects.

What is necessary to make macro photography? There are lots of roads to nice results, here listed from cheaper to more expensive:

- A close-up filter, that make it possible to get close to you subject.
- An extension tube - or a whole set of - that moves the lens further away from the film, thereby allowing you to move closer.
- A bellows that does the same as extension tubes, but does it in a flexible way.
- A macro lens.

In fact there are more solutions, but they are more complicated.

The bellows solution is probably difficult to get your hand on, as not many are on the market for older cameras, and the close-up filter should only be used to find out, if macro is for you, as the quality of images are lousy.

Thus, the recommended way to go is either extension rings or a macro capable lens.

Extension rings can be had for a few bucks, even with electronic connection, if that is something your camera has. The solution is somewhat restricting, as with a specific extension ring you will only be able to focus within limited range. If you need to get further away or closer, you will need to exchange the extension ring or add one more.

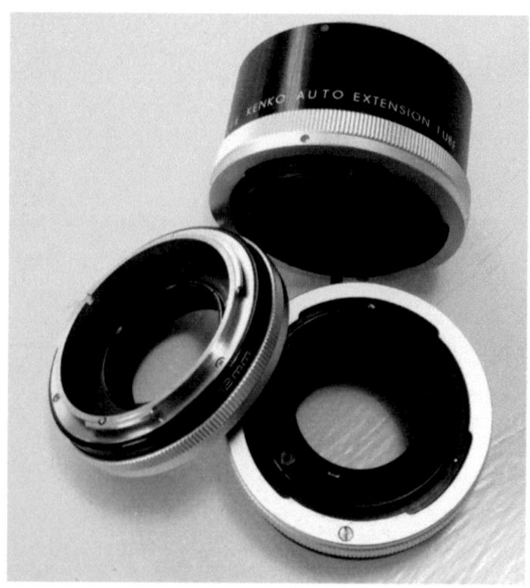

A complete set of extension tubes typically consist of 3 rings. My set for the Canon FD bayonet consist of extension rings of resp. 12mm, 20mm, and 36mm. They are very cheap.

The enlargement that the shortest and the longest provide can be judged from the image series on the next page. First image is shot solely using my Canon 50mm f1.4 that focuses to 45cm. The next two are shot with resp. the 12mm and the 36mm extension tubes.

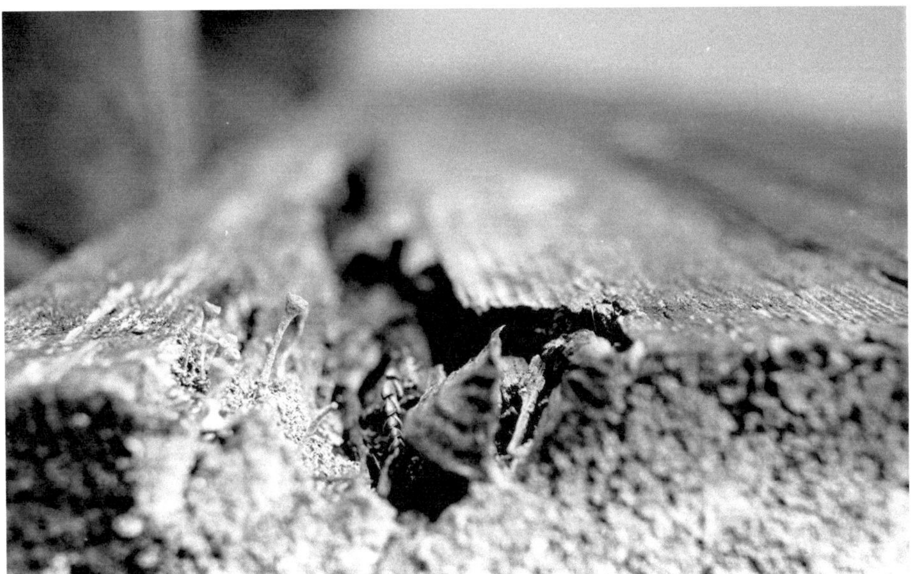

Decent depth of field in a macro photo is a challenge. As you move very close the DOF becomes ridiculously small. The effect is that only a small part of the image is sharp, especially if you need to open up the aperture. The effect is clearly visible in the mushrooms on my rotting stairs, where only a few millimeters are sharp.

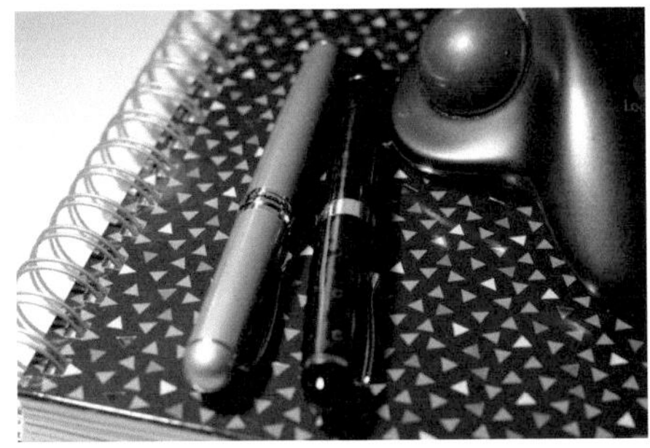

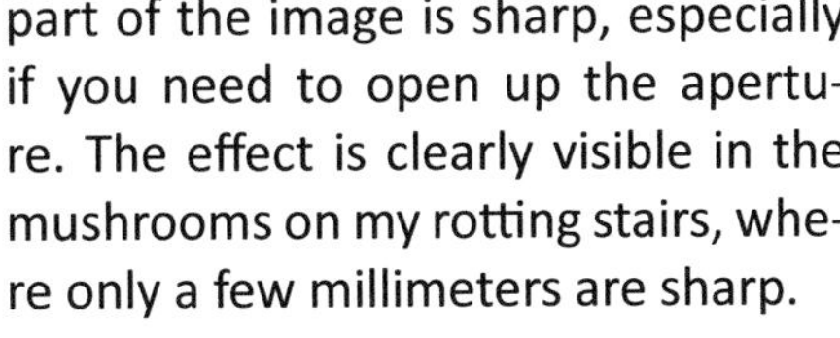

My example with the tree images is shot on aperture 1.4 to show exactly how small the DOF is at very open apertures.

The depth of field can be increased by stopping down, then you'll have a more of your subject in focus, but it creates another challenge. There is

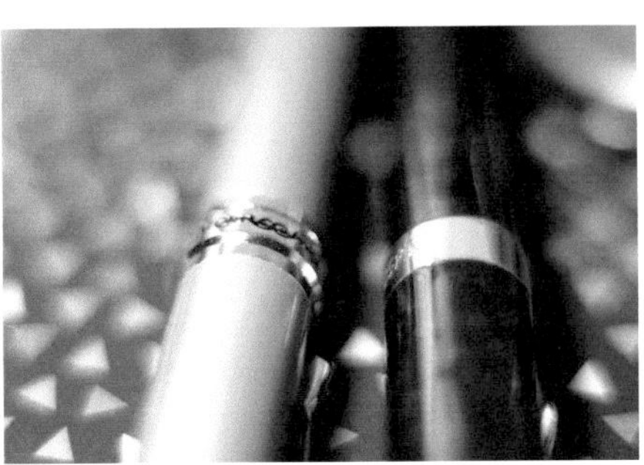

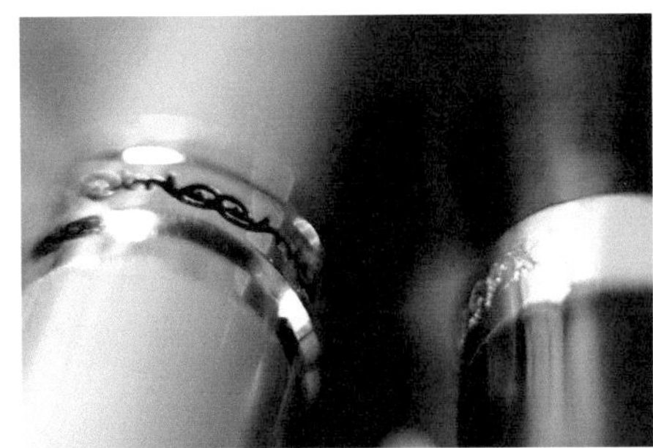

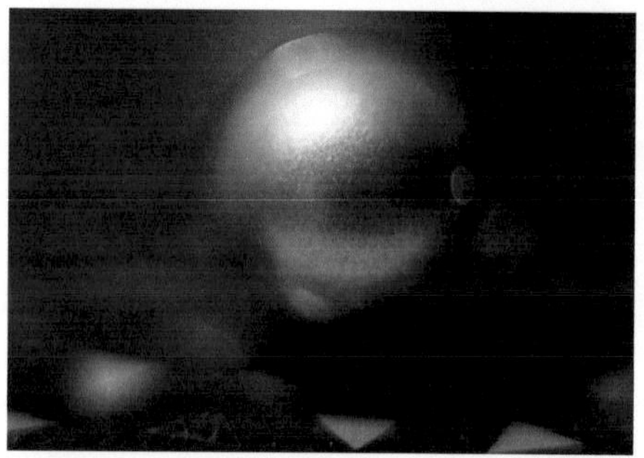

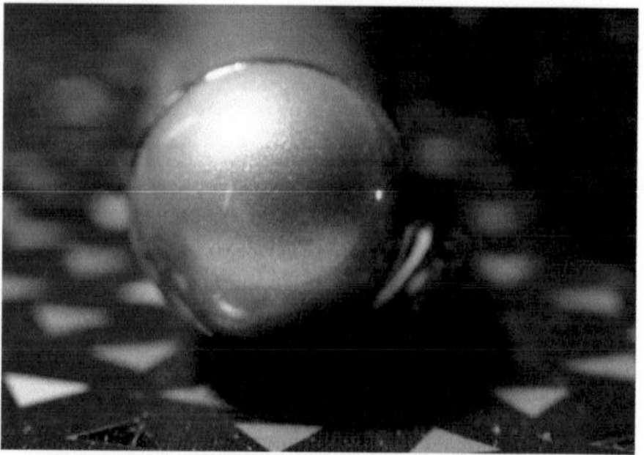

not light enough to secure for camera shake.

The example above shows, how the DOF can be increased by stopping down from f1.4 to f16.

A macro lens is probably the best solution, and there are a number of zoom lenses, that can get pretty close without being real macro lenses. My own macro lens go all the way to 1:1 reproduction, and by using an extension ring I can obtain enlargement of up to 4-5 times. It is a newer lens, that works equally well with my older analog cameras as well as with my digital cameras. It is a very flexible solution, that furthermore doubles as a very good portrait lens.

The images at the bottom of the page shows how close you often can get with a normal lens. Some can get a bit closer than others, but it is the typical close focus of 40-50cm. Some of the

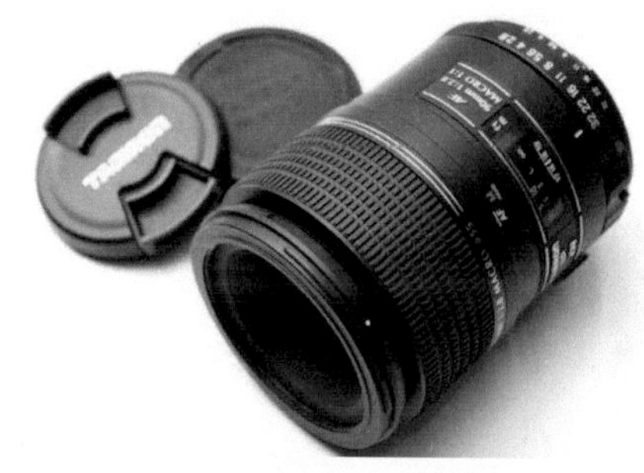

older zoom lenses can even go closer, or be used at the same distance but with a longer focal length. Thereby, you will also get higher magnification.

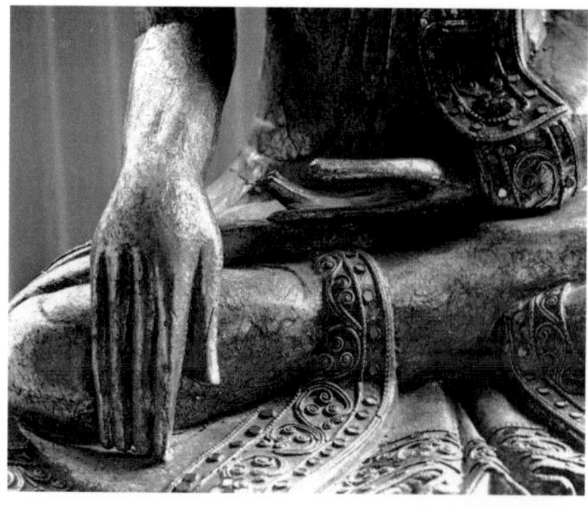

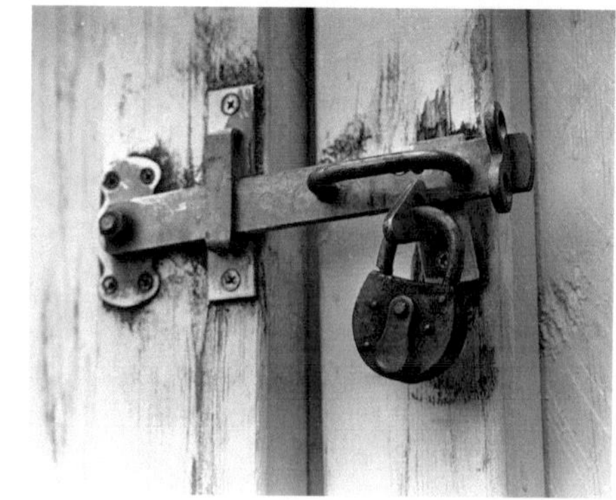

Double exposure

Holga cameras, as low tech as they are, completely changed the perception of, what an interesting camera is. Double exposures became a necessary feature, ie. more than one exposure on the same film frame, and Holgas made it easy due to the lack of any kind of exposure blocking. Many started using this "feature" creatively.

Personally, I haven't explored this very much, but I have some technical considerations, that you need to remember, if you want to enter this very creative territory.

First of all, most cameras except some very old make sure you don't accidentally expose twice on the same frame. Therefore, you have to find a way to bypass the double exposure blocking, you're in luck, if you have an older camera without.

Some more advanced cameras like the Nikon FM2 has a small lever, that you pull while cocking the shutter. The camera then doesn't advance the film.

Most manual advance cameras has a button to allow return spooling the film, you have to press this while cocking the shutter, and holding the

My sprocket rocket camera, that you'we seen images from earlier, is a camera, that provides many creative features apart from shooting in a panoramic format.

Double exposure is no problem, as there is no mechanism blocking your ability to take multiple exposures on the same frame. You actually have to be aware, if you don't want double exposure.

Below is a triple exposure of some statues and buildings by the Eremitage castle in Dyrehaven north of Copenhagen.

return spool lever tight to hold the film. You also have to make sure, the camera advances the film, after your double exposure is done. Otherwise you will have triple or more exposures.

Not all cameras can make double exposures. You have to try the described techniques, to find what works.

As you are exposing the same part of the film more than one time, you have to compensate the exposure for this. The calculation you must do is, that every time the number of exposures doubles, the exposure must be halved.

Let's again go with an example. You want a double exposure, and the light meter indicates correct exposure at f8 and 1/125 second. You can now either choose to expose two times at f8 and 1/250 second or two times at f11 and 1/125 second. Both exposures will give half as much light to the film at every exposure.

If you are doing a 4-double exposure, the values will be either 4 exposures at f8 and 1/500 second or f16 and 1/125 second.

It'll be a little more difficult if you want to expose 3 times on the same frame, as you can't use the rule of halving the exposure. You must choose values somewhere in between.

We have now come to the end of, what I wanted you to know in the introduction to analog photography. There is a lot more to explore and learn, and I bid you great pleasure on the journey.

Double exposure with a model and a double wall light. The contrast in the image is not great, but i think the idea behind the image is quite obvious :-)

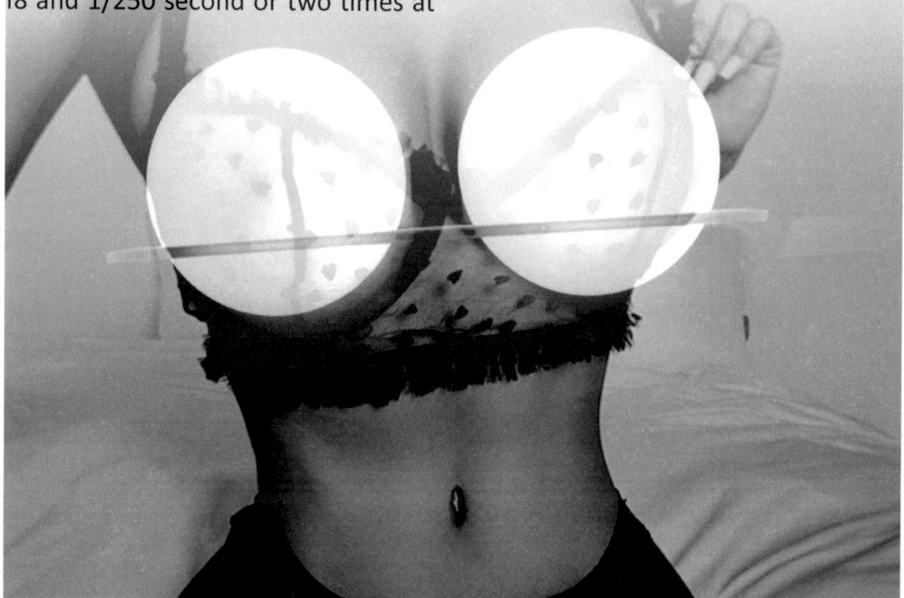

Word list and abbreviations

If you want to learn more, and read articles on the internet, or watch youtube videos there's a lot of abbreviations and terms in use. Here is a collection of the most used terms and a short explanation of their meaning. I have introduced most of them in the book, but I think it's a good idea to have a complete list.

Some of the abbreviations are camera manufacturer dependent, and I have tried to include them all, but might have missed some.

Feature, functionality, or photographic field	Abbreviation (if any) and explanation
Automatic mode	Auto (often marked with a green indicator or rectangle).
Optical Image Stabilisation Vibration Reduction	OIS (Canon) VR (Nikon)
Aperture	A
Aperture priority	A, Av (Canon)
Depth of Field	DOF, the distance from the nearest object, that can be sharp, to the farthest object, that can be sharp.
The Exposure Triangle	Diagram showing the relation between ISO, aperture, and shutter speed.
Mount	FD (older Canon), EOS (newer Canon), F (Nikon), PK (Pentax K), OL (Olympus), M42 (Old universal screw mount).
Film sensitivity	ISO on new cameras and film - DIN/ASA on older cameras/film.
Landscape	Both an orientation of the camera and a photographic field.
Lens	Optics that project the image to the film.

Shutter	Device that controls how long time light hits the film.
Shutter time	S
Shutter priority	S, Tv (canon)
Portrait	Both an orientation of the camera and a photographic field.
Program mode	P
Screw mount	M42, one of several screw mounts that was almost universally accepted
Street photography	Photographic field.
Unsharpness/Blur	The look of areas not in focus, the effect of camera shake, or a fast moving object not stopped by short shutter time.

The image below is shot on one of the smallest cameras, I have owned, a Rollei 35TE. It is known for its sublime lens, that can be had even better in the 35SE model, but unfortunately they have both become a bit expensive. A nice depth of field in the image has been achieved by using f11. The lens on the 35TE model is a 40mm f3.5 lens, bitingly sharp already from its most open aperture.

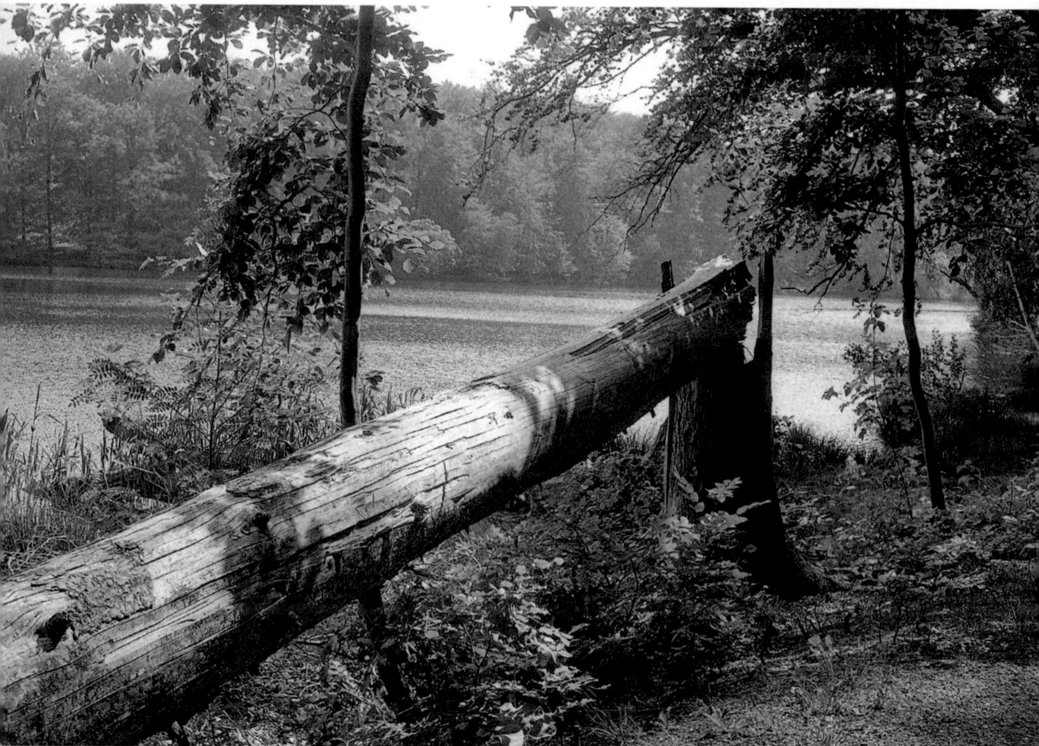

Litterature

The books in the literature list are primarily intended as inspiration to find you own style. I haven't included further books on techniques. My own books provide information on how and using what settings the images are made, in order for you to try out something likewise.

Christensen, Bo Belvedere:

Panoramic Images, Books on Demand, 2021. Photographs in panoramic mode with information on both camera and settings. Includes images from both analog and digital cameras.

Everest Basecamp Trek, Books on Demand, 2020. An image based narrative from the Everest Basecamp trek with information on cameras and technique. Includes images from nature, villages on the route, as well as from Kathmandu, and people both locals and trip participants. Both analog and digital images.

Annapurna Basecamp Trek, Books on Demand, 2020. An image based narrative from the Annapurna Basecamp trek with information on cameras and technique. Includes images from nature, villages on the route, as well as from Kathmandu, and people both locals and trip participants. Both analog and digital images.

Heller, Steven:

A History of Photography. From 1839 to the Present, Taschen, 2019. The history of photography with a load of image examples and the photographers, that was behind the camera. Inspiring book for photographers seeking a vintage look in their images.

James, Christopher:

The Book of Alternative Photographic Processes, Course Technology, 2015. An exhaustive examination of alternative processes for achieving creative, artful results. Aimed at the advanced photographer, this book provides an almost inexhaustible source of alternative and creative approaches to the artistic side of photography.

Kenna, Michael:

Holga, Prestel 2017. The famous photographer Michael Kenna shows with his book, the fantastic images he has crated using the cheap Holga plastic camera, a technically inferior camera that in the hands of an artist can provide amazing results. Very inspiring book.

Images of the Seventh Day, Skira, 2020. Here Michael Kenna demonstrates his mastery in black and white images of landscapes, and often empty streets and houses. The book is a bit gloomy, but at the same time it is beautiful and expressive. It shows how simple images can provide a strong impression.

Klein, Kirsten:

Mellem lyset og mørket (Between light and dark), Gyldendal 2009. Danish book with dramatic and at the same time beautiful images from nature. All images shot on analog cameras, and the way they are composed and exposed give a very special look, a sort of photographic signature unique to Kirsten Klein. Language is Danish, but worth the while for the images.

Koetzle, Hans Michael:

Photographers A-Z, Taschen, 2020. Biographies for a number of the Worlds most renowned photographers. Provides lots of inspiration.

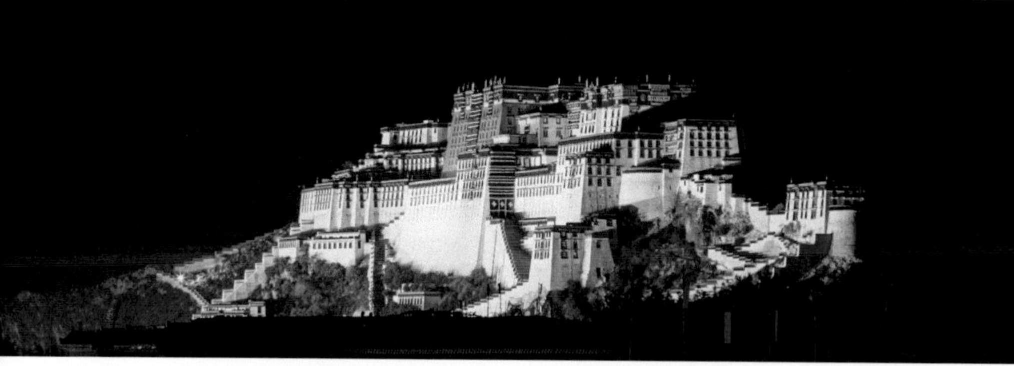

The above is an image of Potala in Lhasa, Tibet. The image avoids magically to show the surrounding Chinese city, that has grown up around Dalai Lamas former residence before the chinese invasion. Potala is shot in the evening using a 200mm lens from the roof terrace of my hotel.

Opposite is a cairn near Ama Dablam basecamp, Nepal. A quiet and beatiful motive photographed using a Canon EF with a 35mm lens on a low aperture value, though I don't recall exactly what.

The image on the next spread is probably one the most succesfull from my climbing career. The snow ridge leads to the summit of Mont Maudit, a sidetop to Mont Blanc. It is shot on a simpel Konica Z-up 70 camera using Konica slide film. Konica doesn't exist anymore, but the camera still works impeccably.

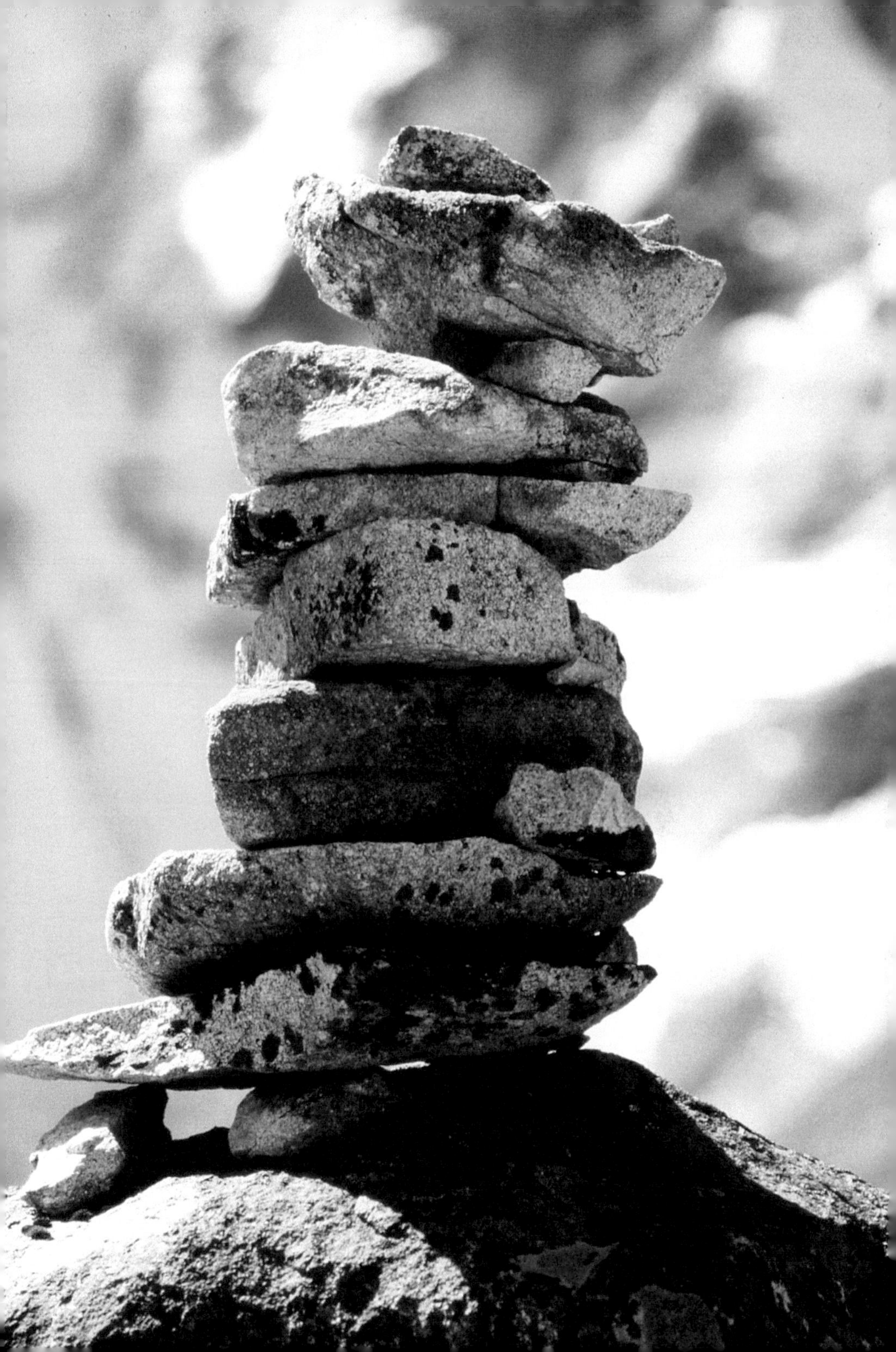

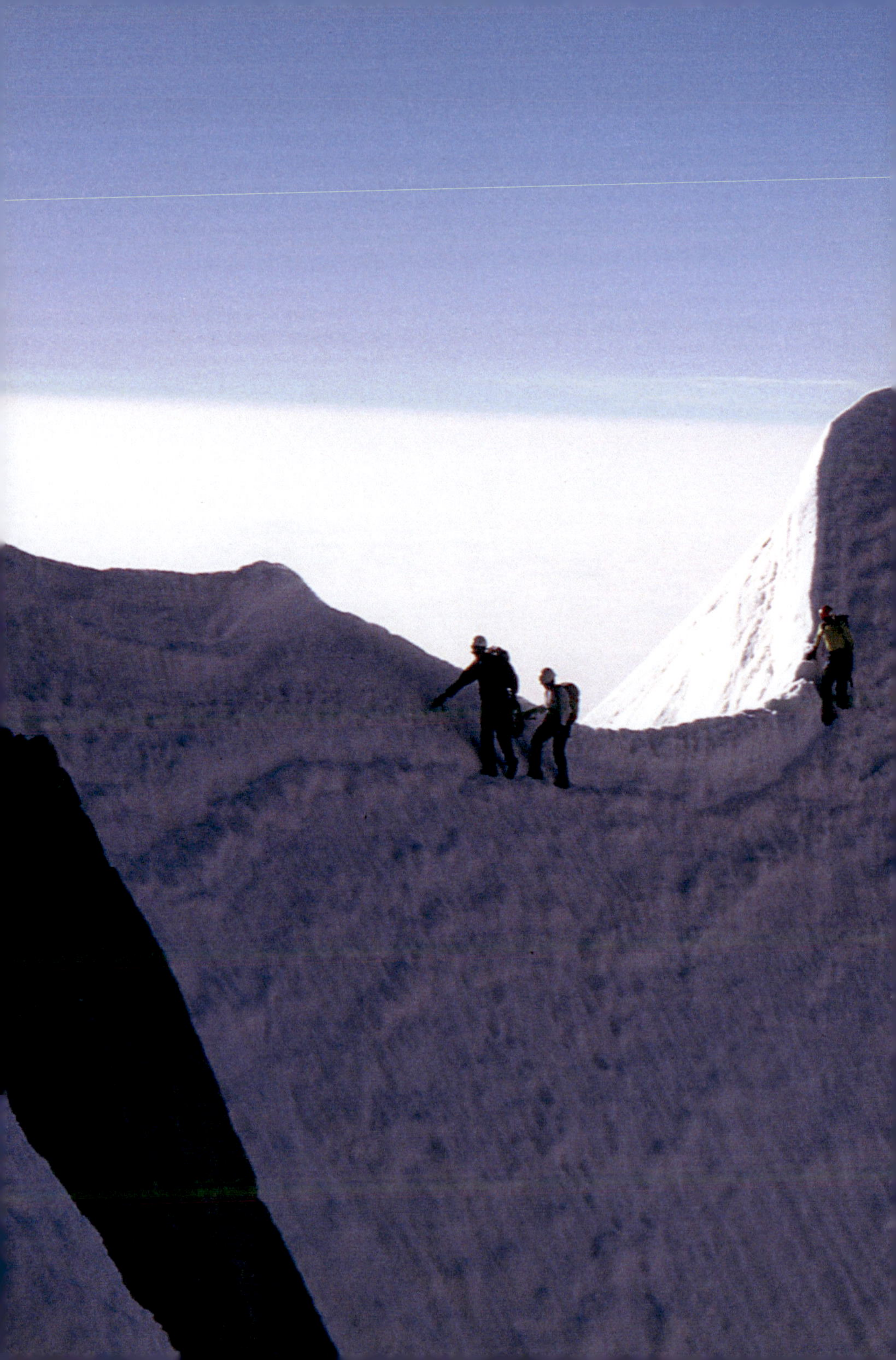

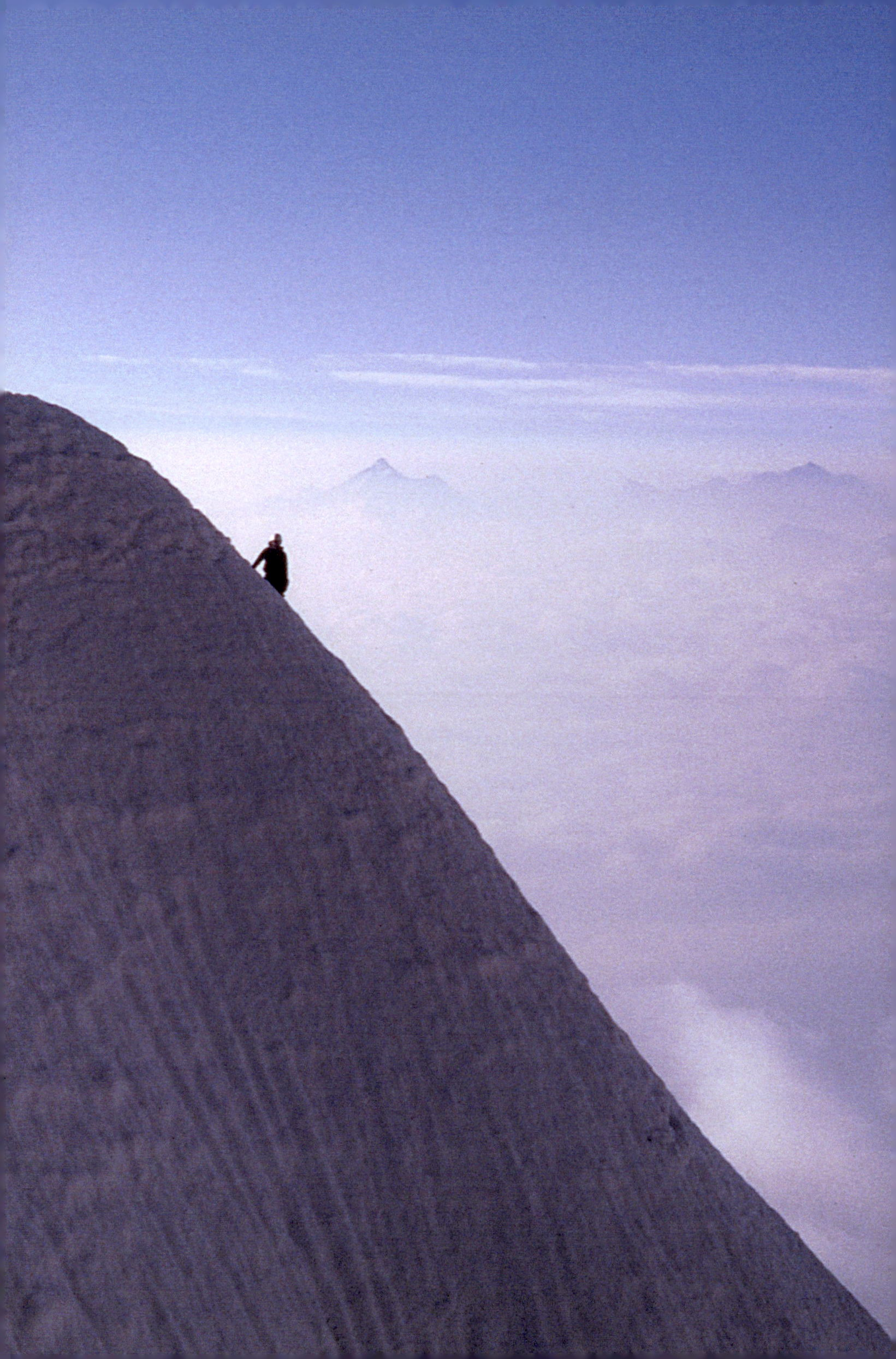